HOME, FAMILY & EVERYDAY LIFE

through the ages

Series Editor DR JOHN HAYWOOD

southwater

This edition is published by Southwater, an imprint of Anness Publishing Limited, Hermes House, 88–89 Blackfriars Road, London SE1 8HA; tel. 020 7401 2077; fax 020 7633 9499 www.southwaterbooks.com; www.annesspublishing.com

If you like the images in this book and would like to investigate using them for publishing, promotions or advertising, visit our website www.practicalpictures.com for more information.

UK agent: The Manning Partnership Ltd; tel. 01225 478444; fax 01225 478440; sales@manning-partnership.co.uk
UK distributor: Grantham Book Services Ltd; tel. 01476 541080; fax 01476 541061; orders@gbs.tbs-ltd.co.uk
North American agent/distributor: National Book Network; tel. 301 459 3366; fax 301 429 5746; www.nbnbooks.com
Australian agent/distributor: Pan Macmillan Australia; tel. 1300 135 113; fax 1300 135 103; customer.service@macmillan.com.au
New Zealand agent/distributor: David Bateman Ltd; tel. (09) 415 7664; fax (09) 415 8892

ETHICAL TRADING POLICY
Because of our ongoing ecological investment programme, you, as our customer, can have the pleasure and reassurance of knowing that a tree is being cultivated on your behalf to naturally replace the materials used to make the book you are holding. For further information about this scheme, go to www.annesspublishing.com/trees

Publisher Joanna Lorenz
Managing Editor, Children's Books Gilly Cameron Cooper
Project Editor Rasha Elsaeed
Editorial Reader Jonathan Marshall
"From Shelters to Homes" Introduction by Fiona Macdonald
Authors Daud Ali, Jen Green, Charlotte Hurdman, Fiona Macdonald, Lorna Oakes, Philip Steele, Michael Stotter, Richard Tames
Consultants Nick Allen, Cherry Alexander, Clara Bezanilla, Felicity Cobbing, Penny Dransart, Jenny Hall, Dr John Haywood, Dr Robin Holgate, Michael Johnson, Lloyd Laing, Jessie Lim, Heidi Potter, Louise Schofield, Leslie Webster.
Designers Simon Borrough, Matthew Cook, Joyce Mason, Caroline Reeves, Margaret Sadler, Alison Walker, Stuart Watkinson at Ideas Into Print, Sarah Williams
Special Photography John Freeman
Stylists Konika Shakar, Thomasina Smith, Melanie Williams

Previously published as part of the Step Into series in 14 separate volumes: Ancient Egypt, Ancient Greece, Ancient India, Ancient Japan, Arctic World, Aztec & Maya Worlds, Celtic World, Chinese Empire, Inca World, Mesopotamia, North American Indians, Roman Empire, Viking World, The Stone Age.

PICTURE CREDITS (b=bottom, t=top, c=center, l=left, r=right)
Lesley & Roy Adkins Picture Library: 35bl; AKG: 10b, 11tl, 18c, 19tl, 44bl; B & C Alexander: title page 48cl, 49cl & 49tr, 50cl, 51c, 52cl & 52cr, 53tr & 53cl; The Ancient Art & Architecture Collection Ltd: 12, 13bl, 14b, 15bc, 23br, 28tr, 32tr & 32bl, 35bl, 43tr; Andes Press Agency: 61bl; GDR Barnett Images: 54tl; The Bodleian Library: 56bl, 57bl; A-Z Botanical Collection Ltd: 33r; Bildarchiv Preussischer Kulturbesitz: 10t, 11br; The Bridgeman Art Library: 43l; The British Museum: 13tr, 14t, 15tr, 32br, 34l; Bulloz: 10m; Jean-Loup Charmet: 28cl, 29tr, 30l; Peter Clayton: 28cl, 29tr, 30l; Corbis: 14tr, 16tr, 18tl, 19cl, 44br, 45cl, 46c, 51tl; Sue Cunningham Photographic: 59tl & 59tr; C M Dixon: front cover, 8tl & 8b, 9bl & 9br, 13tl, 15tl, 27cl, 34r, 36tl & 36c, 37tr & 37c, 38cr, 39tl & 39cl, 41tr, 43tl, 46cl & 47tr, 47cl, 56tl; E T Archive: 3, 7tc, 22tr & 22bl, 23bl, 24tr, 25tr, 26tl, 27tr, 40bl, 43br, 54tr; Mary Evans Picture Library: 22br, 53tl, 57br; Werner Forman Archive: 24cr, 33t, 41tl, 57tr, 60t & 60br; Robert Harding: 11tr, 14b, 15bl, 16b, 17bl, 41bl, 43c; MacQuitty Collections: 25cl; Michael Holford: 28tl, 29tl, 33bl; National Museum of Scotland: 37cl; Peter Newark: 44tr, 45tl, 47tl & 47tr; NHPA: 27c; Planet Earth: 48tl, 50tl, 58b; South American Photo Library: 26bl, 54cl, 58t, 60bl; Statens Historic Museum: 42tr; Tony Stone: 51tr; Visual Arts Library: 23tr, 26tl; Keith Welch: 37tl; York University Trust: 40tr, 41br, 42b; ZEFA: 21tr

CONTENTS

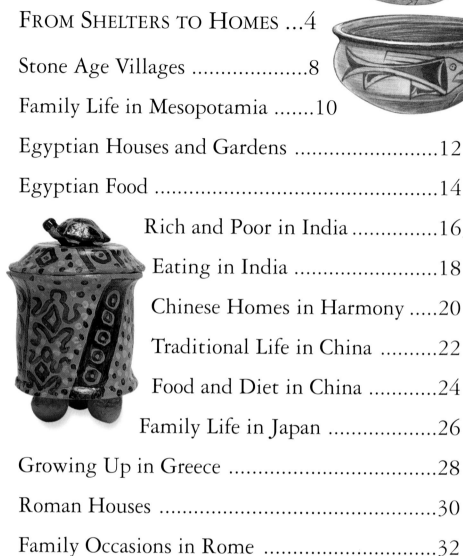

KEY

Look for the patterns used throughout this book, there is one for each culture

The Stone Age

Mesopotamia

Ancient Egypt

India

China

Japan

Ancient Greece

Roman Empire

The Celts

The Vikings

North American

Indians

The Arctic

Aztec & Maya

Inca Empire

From Shelters to Homes

Everyone needs somewhere to live. All over the world, people from different civilizations have built many kinds of homes. From the simplest prehistoric cave-shelters, to the most splendid palaces in Mughal India, a home serves many purposes that are common in all cultures. They provided protection from cold and damp, shade from the hot sun, and comfortable refuge for sleeping, preparing food, raising a family, and entertaining guests.

The layout and construction of houses varied widely. Homes were designed to provide maximum comfort in the local climate, and to withstand local environmental hazards, such as storms, floods, earthquakes, and heavy snow. In northern Europe, the Vikings built houses with thick thatched roofs for insulation from the cold. In Japan, an earthquake zone, lightweight paper screens were used as inner walls in the construction of houses. If these collapsed, they

Round, early farming huts, such as this one, whose remains were found in Banpo in China, date from 6000 B.C. They had wooden frames, plastered walls, and a hole to let out smoke.

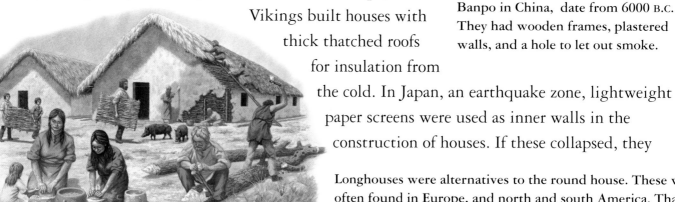

Longhouses were alternatives to the round house. These were often found in Europe, and north and south America. Thatch made from reeds from a nearby river lasted longer than straw.

Timeline 10,000–200 B.C.

10,000 B.C. People around the world live as nomads, moving from place to place, hunting animals and gathering wild foods. They shelter in strong, solid houses, made of wood, stone, or snow in winter, but travel around, living in tents in summer. Seminomadic lifestyle continues until the 1900s in places such as arctic Russia.

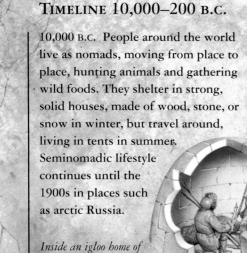

Inside an igloo home of the Arctic Inuit people

10,000 B.C. People living in north and south America develop homes according to the local environment. Some are simple shelters of branches and leaves; others include earth lodges, longhouses made of woven saplings, buffalo-skin tipis, and mud-brick pueblo apartments.

8000–7000 B.C. The world's first settled farming villages are built in the Middle East.

4500 B.C. European farmers build villages of longhouses.

3100–30 B.C. The peak of ancient Egyptian civilization. Egyptians live in houses made of sun-dried mud brick.

European longhouse village

800 B.C.–A.D. 100 The Celts in central and northwestern Europe live as

10,000 B.C.   4500 B.C.   3000 B.

would not harm people and cause much damage.

The materials used to construct a house also shaped its design. Most homes were built using local resources that were easily available. In many countries, including Aztec Mexico and ancient Egypt, mud and clay were shaped into bricks and dried in the sun. Elsewhere, homes were made from wood, stone, and dried grass. Fine stone and timber were rare, and it was difficult to carry them long distances, so they were expensive. The materials used and the size of homes depended on the wealth of the owner. Houses of the wealthy were large and luxurious, with many spacious rooms. Among the poor, all family members might share a simple room that combined as sleeping and living space.

Houses were built on stilts in the marshy regions of Japan, where rice was cultivated in wet paddy fields.

Most homes were built as permanent shelters, but in some environments, they were designed to fulfill temporary needs. Nomads were people who moved from place to place, hunting animals and gathering wild plants for food. They built homes that were designed to be easily packed away and moved several times a year. Native American hunters on the Great Plains of North America made tipis of buffalo skin. Inuit hunters in the Arctic built shelters from blocks of snow, called igloos,

Tipis made of animal skins were held up with wooden poles, and they served as a short-term shelter for Native American peoples.

farmers, building large roundhouses of wattle-and-daub, thatched with straw. They also build fortified towns as centers of trade.

600 B.C. Wealthy families in India build houses of brick and stone. They are painted different colors, according to caste (social status).

600–200 B.C. Ancient Greek families live in houses made of stone or mud bricks. They have separate, private quarters for women, and a dining room for entertaining, used only by men of the family.

c.300 B.C.–A.D. 300 Wealthy Roman families build splendid houses. Town houses were often built around a small enclosed garden, or a courtyard called an atrium. Country houses had elegant rooms for entertaining, plus barracks where slaves and farmworkers could sleep.

300 B.C. In Central America, the Maya build new cities surrounded by fields and farms. Mayan families live in simple homes, with wood or mud walls and thatched roofs.

A wealthy Roman family home.

00 B.C.   400 B.C.   300 B.C.   200 B.C.

to live in during the long winter months.

For many people, homes were also places of work. From the time when humans first began to live together in families, women worked at home, caring for babies and young children. In most cultures, women did the cooking and produced household textiles, such as blankets and clothes, for their families. Archaeologists have found children's toys, cooking pots, and the remains of weaving looms in family homes from places as diverse as India and Incan Peru. Men, who made their living as farmers and craftspeople, also worked at home, with other family members helping them. Teamwork was essential for survival. Children worked alongside their parents, learning the skills they would need in adult life. School was only provided for children from wealthy families, as in China and imperial Rome.

Backstrap looms started to be used as early as 2500 B.C. by the people who lived in the Andes mountains of Peru.

All these family and working needs were reflected in house designs. Craft workshops, rooms to display finished goods, and shelters for farm animals often formed part of the family home. Cultural values also influenced housing. In ancient Greece, homes had private rooms where women lived, out of the sight of

Homelife in early Middle Eastern farming villages was a cluster of activity. People often shared their house with the animals. Everyone in the family had a role to play.

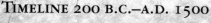

TIMELINE 200 B.C.–A.D. 1500

206 B.C.–A.D. 220 The Han dynasty rules China. Large, extended families live in courtyard homes, with many different rooms surrounded by strong walls, and guarded by gates and a watchtower.

A.D. 1–1000 The Dorset people of the North American Arctic live as nomad hunters in the summer and in snow-house villages during the winter.

A Chinese Han dynasty house

A.D. 700–1100 The Vikings from Scandinavia build new settlements in many European lands, also in Iceland, Greenland, and North America. Viking homes are built to withstand the cold, with thick roofs and walls. Depending on the site, they are built from stone, wood and thatch, or turf.

710 The Nara empire comes to power in Japan. They built a splendid new capital city at Nara.

200 B.C.   A.D. 100   700   800

nonfamily men. Almost everywhere, people liked to decorate their houses, sometimes in bright colors and patterns, and to furnish them with comfortable bedding, seating, and floor-coverings. Some of these decorations had a meaning, with the aim of protecting a house or watching over those who lived there. Chinese families often displayed a picture of the kitchen god, who monitored their behavior. Some Native Americans put up tall totem poles outside their homes, carved with images of ancestor spirits, to guard the families.

In every Chinese kitchen, a new paper picture of the kitchen god and his wife was put up on New Year's Day.

This book charts the development of domestic history in various cultures in turn. It focuses on aspects of everyday life that are common to major civilizations, such as family, childhood, education, housing, and food. You will be able to see how these themes evolved and compare how people's lives varied with local environments around the world.

An Aztec couple sit by the fire, while their meal is being cooked. Their colorful clothes and braided hair indicate that they are people of rank.

Wooden totem poles outside Native American homes kept a record of the family histories of the people living inside.

1000–1325 The Aztec people of Central America leave their homeland in the north of Mexico, and travel south in search of a better place to live. They settle in the central valley of Mexico and build a new capital city Tenochtitlan. It soon grows into one of the largest cities in the world.

1000–1600 The Thule people of the North American Arctic live in huts made of stone and turf.

Inca man and woman gather straw for thatch

*c.*1300–1536 The Inca Empire is powerful in Peru. The Incas are expert builders, of stone temples, palaces, and city walls, without using metal tools. Ordinary families live in small stone houses, thatched with straw.

1500 In Japan, samurai (noble warriors) build splendid castles where their servants, soldiers, and families live.

An Incan home

1000

1300

1500

Stone Age Villages

PRIMITIVE HUMANS hunted wild animals, caught fish, and gathered berries and plants to eat. When people took up farming as a way of life, it meant that they had to stay in the same place for a long time. Some farmers practiced slash and burn. This means that they cleared the land, but moved after a few years, when their crops had exhausted the soil. Elsewhere, early farming settlements grew into villages five to ten times bigger than earlier hunter-gatherer camps. At first, the farmers still hunted animals, but soon their herds and crops supplied most of their needs. They lived in villages of rectangular or circular one-story houses made from stone, mud brick, or timber and thatch. Houses were connected by narrow lanes and courtyards. Most villages lay near well-watered, easily worked land. By using irrigation and crop rotation, later farmers were able to stay in one place for a long time.

INSIDE A LONGHOUSE
The inside of a longhouse was a place of work, and it also provided shelter for the family and their animals. Around the hearth of this reconstructed house are baskets woven from reeds and skins laid out the floor. Tools are stored around the walls.

A LONGHOUSE
This is a reconstruction of a typical longhouse in an early farming village in Europe. The village dates from around 4500 B.C.

A TOWN HOUSE

This picture shows how a house at Çatal Hüyük in Turkey may have looked. The walls were made of mud brick, with a roof made from poles covered with reeds and mud. All the houses were joined together, with no streets in between. People got around by climbing over the rooftops, entering their homes by a ladder through the roof.

The main room of each house had raised areas for sitting and sleeping. More than a thousand houses were packed together like this one at Çatal Hüyük.

STONE WALLS

These are the remains of the walls of a house in an early farming village in Jordan. It was built around 7000 B.C. The walls are made from stone collected from the local area.

The first farming towns and villages appeared in the Near East. Most were built from mud brick, and over hundreds of years, such settlements were often rebuilt many times on the same site.

THE OVEN

Many houses contained ovens or kilns, used for baking bread and firing pottery. A kiln allowed higher temperatures to be reached than an open hearth, and therefore produced better pottery. Each village probably made its own pottery.

Family Life in Mesopotamia

LIFE WAS HARD for ordinary families in Mesopotamia. Many babies and young children died from disease, or because of poor maternity care. Boys from poorer families did not go to school, but worked with their fathers, who taught them their trades. Girls stayed at home with their mothers—they learned how to keep house and helped to take care of the younger children. Some of the details of family life are described in ancient clay tablets. In one tablet, a boy rudely tells his mother to hurry up and make his lunch. In another one, a boy is scared of what his father will say when he sees his bad school report.

In some ways, Mesopotamian society was quite modern. The law said that women could own property and get a divorce. However, if a woman was unable to have a baby for any reason, she had to agree to her husband taking a second wife. The second wife and her children had rights, too. They remained part of the household, even if the first wife had a child eventually.

MOTHERHOOD
Having lots of healthy children, especially sons, was very important, because families needed children to grow up and work for them. Most women stayed at home to take care of their families. Women did not usually go out to work, although some had jobs as priestesses. Some priestesses were single, but others were married women.

HOUSEHOLD GOODS
Pottery was used in Mesopotamian homes from the time of the first villages. At first it was handmade, but later, a potter's wheel was used. This clay jug may have been based on one made of metal. Tools and utensils were made of stone or metal. There was not much furniture in a Mesopotamian house—just mud brick benches for sitting or sleeping on. There may have been rugs and cushions to make the homes more comfortable, but none have survived.

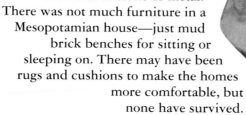

MODEL HOUSE
From models such as this one, we know that homes in Mesopotamia were similar to village houses in modern Iraq. They were built from mud brick and were usually rectangular, with rooms around a central courtyard. Doors and windows were small to keep the house warm in the cold winters and cool during the hot summers. Flat roofs, which were reached by stairs from the central court, could be used as extra rooms in the summer.

Mesopotamian Fashions

A statue of a worshipper found in a temple shows the dress of a Sumerian woman. Dresses were made from sheepskin, also with a sheepskin shawl, or from woolen cloth. One shoulder was left bare. Some women, who may have been priestesses, wore tall, elaborate hats like this one. Later fashions included long, fringed garments. Sumerian men wore sheepskin kilts, and men in the Assyrian and Babylonian Empires wore long, woolen tunics. Both men and women wore jewelery.

Earning a Living

Most families in ancient Mesopotamia depended on agriculture for a living, just as many people in the Middle East do today. Farmers rented their land from bigger landowners, such as important officials, kings, and temples, and had to give part of what they produced in taxes. Many townspeople had jobs in the local government or worked in the textile and metalwork industries.

Build It Up

Homes in Mesopotamia were often made from mud brick. Mud bricks are made from a mixture of mud and straw mixed with water. The straw stops the bricks from cracking. The mixture is put in square or oblong moulds and left to dry in the sun for several weeks. The bricks are usually made in the summer after the harvest when there is plenty of straw available, and it is less likely to rain (which would damage the bricks).

straw

clay

Gone Fishing

There were lots of fish in the rivers and fishponds of ancient Iraq, and fish seem to have been an important part of people's diet. Fishbones were found at Eridu, in the south of Sumer, in the oldest level of the temple. Perhaps fish were offered to the water god Enki as an offering. (He is the god with streams of water containing fish springing out of his shoulders.) Some of the carved reliefs from the Assyrian palaces give us rare glimpses into everyday life that include little scenes of men going fishing.

Egyptian Houses and Gardens

THE GREAT CITIES of ancient Egypt, such as Memphis and Thebes, were built along the banks of the River Nile. Small towns grew up haphazardly around them. Special workmen's towns, such as Deir el-Medina, were set up around major burial sites and temples to help with building work.

Egyptian towns were defended by thick walls, and the streets were planned on a grid pattern. The straight dirt roads had a stone drainage channel, or gutter, running down the middle. Parts of the town housed important officials, and other parts were home to craftspeople and poor laborers.

Only temples were built to last—they were made of stone. Mud brick was used to construct all other buildings, from royal palaces to workers' dwellings. Most Egyptian homes had roofs supported with palm logs, and floors made of packed earth. In the homes of wealthier Egyptians, walls were sometimes plastered and painted. The rooms of their houses included bedrooms, living rooms, kitchens in thatched courtyards, and workshops. Homes were furnished with beds, chairs, stools, and benches. In the cool of the evenings, people would sit on the flat roofs, or walk and talk in shady gardens.

THE GARDEN OF NAKHT
The royal scribe Nakht and his wife Tjiui take an evening stroll through their garden. Trees and shrubs surround a peaceful pool. Egyptian gardens included date palms, pomegranates, grape vines, scarlet poppies, and blue and pink lotus flowers. Artists in ancient Egypt showed objects in the same picture from different angles, so the trees around Nakht's pool are flattened out.

AN EGYPTIAN HOUSE

You will need: card, pencil, ruler, scissors, white glue, brush, masking tape, acrylic paint (green, white, yellow, red), plaster of Paris, brush, sandpaper, balsa wood, straw, water pot, and brush.

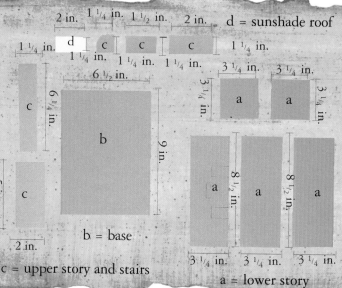

d = sunshade roof

b = base

c = upper story and stairs

a = lower story

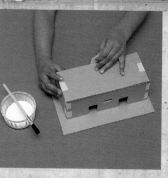

1 Glue together the base board, the walls, and ceiling of the lower story. Reinforce the joints with masking tape. Wait for the glue to dry.

ABOVE THE FLOODS

The homes of wealthy people were often built on platforms to stop damp from passing through the mud brick walls. This also raised it above the level of any possible flood damage.

SOUL HOUSES

Pottery models give us a good idea of how the homes of poorer Egyptians looked. During the Middle Kingdom (2050–1786 B.C.), these soul houses were left as tomb offerings. The Egyptians placed food in the courtyard of the house, to feed the person's soul after death.

NILE SOILS

The Egyptians built their homes from mud bricks that were made from the thick clay soil left behind by the Nile floods. The clay was taken to the brickyard and mixed with water, pebbles, and chopped straw. Mud bricks are still used for building houses in Egypt today, and are made in the same way.

straw

mud

BRICK MAKING

A group of laborers make bricks. First, mud was collected in leather buckets and taken to the building site. There, it was mixed with straw and pebbles. Finally, the mixture was put into a mold. At this stage, bricks were sometimes stamped with the name of the pharaoh or the building for which they were made. They were then left to dry in the hot sunshine for several days, before being transported in a sling.

Egyptian houses had a large main room that opened directly onto the street. In many homes, stairs led up to the roof. People would often sleep there during very hot weather.

2 Now glue together the top story and stairs. Again, use masking tape to reinforce the joints. When the top story is dry, glue it to the lower story.

3 Glue the balsa pillars to the front of the top story. When the house is dry, cover it in wet paste of plaster of Paris. Paint the pillars red or a color of your choice.

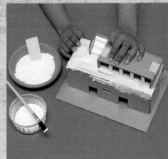

4 Paint the whole building a dried mud color. Next, paint a green strip along the side. Use masking tape to make straight edges. Sand any rough edges.

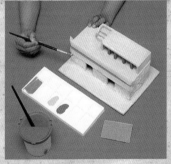

5 Now make a shelter for the rooftop. Use four balsa struts as supports. The roof can be made from card glued with straw. Glue the shelter into place.

Egyptian Food

Laborers in ancient Egypt were often paid in food. They ate bread, onions, and salted fish, washed down with a sweet, grainy beer. Flour was often gritty, and the teeth of many mummified bodies show signs of severe wear and tear. Dough was kneaded with the feet or by hand, and pastry cooks produced all kinds of cakes and loaves.

Beautiful Bowls
Dishes and bowls were often made of faience, a glassy pottery. The usual colors for this attractive tableware was blue-green and turquoise.

A big banquet for a pharaoh was a grand affair, with guests dressed in their finest clothes. A royal menu might include roast goose or stewed beef, kidneys, wild duck, or tender gazelle. For religious reasons, lamb was not eaten, and in some regions certain types of fish were also forbidden. Vegetables such as leeks were stewed with milk and cheese. Egyptian cooks were experts at stewing, roasting, and baking.

Red and white wines were served at banquets. They were stored in pottery jars marked with their year and their vineyard, just like the labels on modern wine bottles.

A Feast Fit for a King
New Kingdom (1550–1070 B.C.) noblewomen exchange gossip at a dinner party. They show off their jewelery and best clothes. Egyptians loved wining and dining. They would be entertained by musicians, dancers, and acrobats during the feast.

Make a Pastry

You will need: $^3/_4$ cip + 1 tbsp. stoneground flour, $^1/_2$ tsp. salt, 1 tsp. baking powder, $^3/_4$ stick butter, 4 tbsp. honey, 3 tbsp. milk, caraway seeds, bowl, wooden spoon, baking tray.

1 Begin by mixing together the flour, salt, and baking powder in the bowl. Next, chop up the butter and add it to the dry ingredients.

2 Using your fingers, rub the butter into the flour, as shown. Your dough should look like fine breadcrumbs when you have finished.

3 Now add $^2/_3$ of your honey. Mix it in with the dough. This will sweeten your pastries. The ancient Egyptians did not have sugar.

WOMAN MAKING BEER

This wooden tomb model of a woman making beer dates back to 2400 B.C. Beer was made by mashing barley bread in water. When the mixture fermented and became alcoholic, the liquid was strained into a wooden tub. There were various types of beer, but all were very popular. It was said that the god Osiris had brought beer to the land of Egypt.

DRINKING VESSEL

Beautiful faience cups such as this one could have been used to drink wine, water, and beer. It is decorated with a pattern of lotus flowers.

DESERT DESSERTS

A meal in ancient Egypt was often completed with nuts, such as almonds, and sweet fruits: juicy figs, dates, grapes, pomegranates, and melons. Sugar was still unknown, so honey was used to sweeten cakes and pastries.

pomegranates   *dates*

PALACE BAKERY

Whole teams of model cooks and bakers were left in some tombs. This was so that a pharaoh could order them to put on a good banquet to entertain his guests in the other world. Models are shown sifting, mixing, and kneading flour, and also making pastries. Most of our knowledge about Egyptian food and cooking comes from the food boxes and offerings left in tombs.

Egyptian pastries were often shaped in spirals like these. Other popular shapes were rings, like doughnuts, and pyramids. Some were shaped like crocodiles!

4 Add the milk and stir the dough until it is smooth. Roll your dough into a ball, and place it on a floured board or surface. Divide the dough into three.

5 Roll the dough into long strips, as shown. Take a strip and coil it into a spiral to make one pastry. Make the other pastries in the same way.

6 Now sprinkle each pastry with caraway seeds and place them all on a greased baking tray. Complete by glazing the pastries carefully with a little extra honey.

7 Ask an adult to bake them in an oven at 350°F for 20 minutes. When they are ready, take them out and leave on a baking rack to cool.

Rich and Poor in India

Houses in India differed according to social class. Poor people made their homes out of mud, clay, and thatch. Materials such as these do not last long, so few of these houses have survived. By about 600 B.C., wealthier people were building homes made of brick and stone. It is thought that people's caste (class) determined not only the part of a town or city that they lived in, but also what color they painted their homes. The Brahmins (priests caste) of Jodhpur in Rajasthan, for example, painted their houses blue.

A wealthy man's house of about A.D. 400 had a courtyard and an outer room where guests were entertained. Behind this were the inner rooms where the women of the house stayed and where food was cooked. Beyond the house itself, there were often gardens and fountains surrounded by an outside wall. Homes like this stayed much the same in design over many centuries.

Royal palaces were more elaborate. They had many courtyards, and enclosures surrounded by numerous walls. These were to protect the king from beggars and servants who might make a nuisance of themselves. Unlike ordinary homes, palaces changed in design with each new wave of rulers.

DECORATED DOORSTEP
Pictures in chalk and rice powder were drawn on the doorsteps of houses. Over time, they came to signify prosperity and good luck. Making such drawings was one of 64 forms of art that a cultured person was expected to be able to do.

birdcage

mango leaves hung for good luck

water trough

courtyard

MOUNTAIN HOMES
These modern mountain homes made from mud and thatch continue a tradition that is thousands of years old. Unlike valley homes, they have to be well insulated for protection against the colder climate.

THE GOOD LIFE
Life in a rich man's household was divided between the inner area, where he slept and ate, and the outer regions, dominated by a courtyard where he entertained friends, read, listened to music, and strolled in the garden. Here, salons (groups) of men would meet to discuss life and politics.

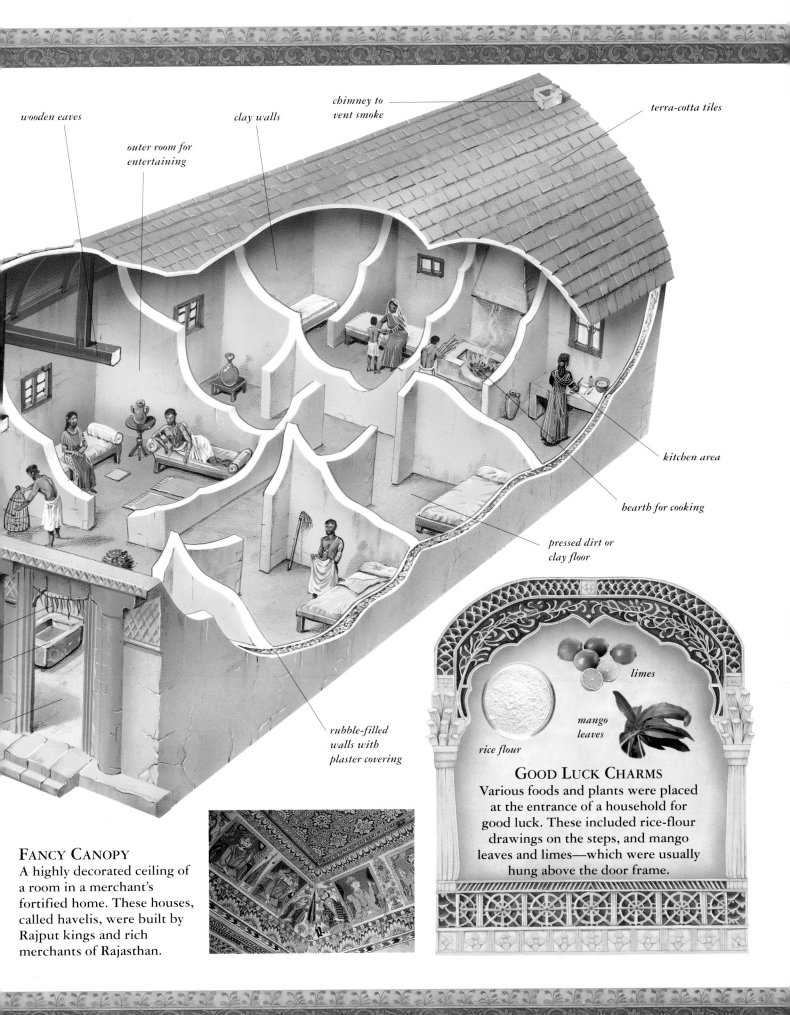

wooden eaves

outer room for
entertaining

clay walls

chimney to
vent smoke

terra-cotta tiles

kitchen area

hearth for cooking

pressed dirt or
clay floor

rubble-filled
walls with
plaster covering

FANCY CANOPY
A highly decorated ceiling of
a room in a merchant's
fortified home. These houses,
called havelis, were built by
Rajput kings and rich
merchants of Rajasthan.

limes

mango
leaves

rice flour

GOOD LUCK CHARMS
Various foods and plants were placed
at the entrance of a household for
good luck. These included rice-flour
drawings on the steps, and mango
leaves and limes—which were usually
hung above the door frame.

Eating in India

PEOPLE'S STAPLE (BASIC) FOODS in the ancient world depended on what they could grow. In the wetter areas of eastern, western, southern, and central India, rice was the staple diet. In the drier areas of the north and northwest, people grew wheat and made it into different kinds of breads.

Apart from these staple foods, people's diets depended on their religion. Buddhists thought that killing animals was wrong, so they were vegetarians. Most Hindus, particularly the upper castes, became vegetarian, too. Because they believed that the cow was holy, eating beef became taboo (forbidden). When Islam arrived, it brought with it a new set of rules. Muslims are forbidden to eat pork, although they do eat other meat.

The Indians used a lot of spices in cooking, in order to add flavor and to disguise the taste of rotten meat. Ginger, garlic, turmeric, cinnamon, and cumin were used from early times. Chilis were only introduced from the Americas after the 1500s.

CELESTIAL FRUITS
A heavenly damsel offers fruits in this stucco painting from Sri Lanka. From earliest times, Indians ate with their hands rather than with implements. Even so, there were rules to be followed. Generally, they could only eat with the right hand, taking care only to use their fingers.

EVENING DELIGHTS
A princess enjoys an evening party in the garden. She listens to music by candlelight, and is served drinks, sweets, and other foods.

MAKE A CHICKPEA CURRY

You will need: knife, a small onion, 2 tsbp. vegetable oil, wok or frying pan, wooden spoon, 1 ¹/₂ in. piece fresh ginger root, 2 cloves garlic, ¹/₄ tsp. turmeric, 1 lb. tomatoes, ¹/₂ lb. cooked chickpeas, salt and pepper, 2 tbsp. finely chopped fresh coriander, plus coriander leaves to garnish, 2 tsp. garam masala, a lime.

1 Chop the onion finely. Heat the vegetable oil in a wok. Fry the onion in the oil for two to three minutes, until it is soft. Ask an adult to help you.

2 Chop the ginger finely and add to the pan. Chop the garlic clove and add it, along with the turmeric. Cook gently for another half a minute.

A Rich Banquet

Babur, the founder of the Mughal Empire in India in A.D. 1526, enjoys a banquet of roast duck in Herat, Persia. Under the Mughals, a cuisine known as Mughlai developed. It became famous for its rich and sophisticated flavors.

turmeric

black mustard seeds

cardamom

Three Essential Spices

Many spices are used in Indian dishes. Turmeric is ground from a root to give food an earthy flavor and yellow color. Black mustard seed has a smoky, bitter taste. Cardamom—a favorite in northern India—gives a musky, sugary flavor that is suitable for both sweet and savory dishes.

Leaf Plate

In southern India, banana leaves were (and are still) used as plates for serving and eating food. Southern Indian food uses more coconut than the north, and rice flour is used in several dishes.

Daily Bread

Indians eat a variety of baked, griddled, and fried breads, such as these parathas. In much of northern and western India, the staple food is wheat, which is baked into unleavened (flat) breads.

Chickpeas are a popular ingredient in Indian cooking. They have been grown in India for thousands of years.

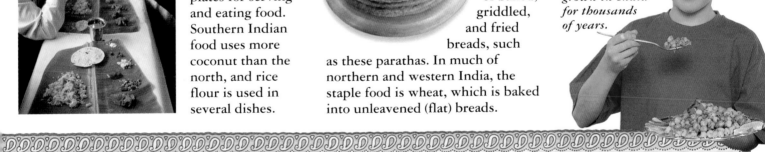

3 Peel the tomatoes, cut them in half, and remove the seeds. Then chop them roughly and add them to the onion, garlic, and spice mixture.

4 Add the chickpeas. Bring to a boil, then simmer gently for 10–15 minutes, until the tomatoes have reduced to a thick paste.

5 Taste the curry, and then add salt and pepper as seasoning, if it is needed. The curry should taste spicy, but not so hot that it burns your mouth.

6 Add the chopped fresh coriander to the curry, along with the garam masala. Garnish with fresh coriander leaves, and serve with slices of lime.

Chinese Homes in Harmony

IN CHINESE CITIES, all buildings were designed to be in harmony with each other and with nature. The direction they faced, their layout, and their proportions were all matters of great spiritual importance. Even the number of steps leading up to the entrance of the house was considered to be significant. House design in imperial China, before it became a republic in 1912, varied over time and between regions. In the hot and rainy south, courtyards tended to be covered for shade and shelter. In the drier north, courtyards were mostly open to the elements. Poor people in the countryside lived in simple, thatched huts. These were made from timber frames covered in mud plaster. They were often noisy, drafty, and overcrowded. In contrast, wealthy people had large, peaceful, and well-constructed homes. Many had beautiful gardens, filled with peonies, bamboo, and wisteria. Some gardens also contained orchards, ponds, and pavilions.

reception

living quarters for owner's immediate family

watchtower

main courtyard

INSIDE A HAN HOUSE

A wealthy family go about their daily lives in a Han dynasty (206 B.C.–A.D. 220) home. The house is built around several courtyards, with a garden at the side and a gatehouse leading into the streets. A watchtower gives a view of the world outside. The main family building at the rear is two stories high, but some homes had three or more floors.

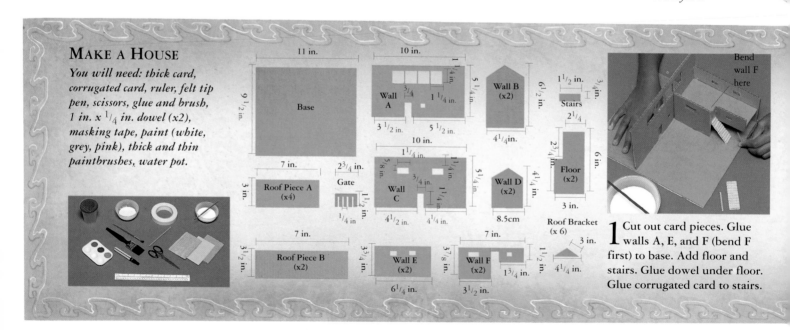

MAKE A HOUSE

You will need: thick card, corrugated card, ruler, felt tip pen, scissors, glue and brush, 1 in. x ¼ in. dowel (x2), masking tape, paint (white, grey, pink), thick and thin paintbrushes, water pot.

Base — 11 in. x 9½ in.

Wall A — 10 in., ¼ in., 5½ in., ¾, 1¼ in., 3½ in., 5½ in.

Wall B (x2) — 6½ in., 4¼ in.

Stairs — 1½ in., ¾ in., 2¼

Bend wall F here

Roof Piece A (x4) — 7 in. x 3 in.

Gate — 2¾ in., 1¼ in., ¼ in.

Wall C — 10 in., 1¼ in., 5⅛ in., ¾ in., 1¼ in., 5¼ in., 4½ in. / 4¼ in.

Wall D (x2) — 4¼ in., 8.5cm

Floor (x2) — 2¾, 6 in., 3 in.

Roof Bracket (x6) — 3 in., 1½ in.

Roof Piece B (x2) — 7 in. x 3½ in.

Wall E (x2) — 3¾ in., 6½ in.

Wall F (x2) — 3⅞ in., 7 in., 1¾ in., 3½ in., 1½ in., 4¼ in.

1 Cut out card pieces. Glue walls A, E, and F (bend F first) to base. Add floor and stairs. Glue dowel under floor. Glue corrugated card to stairs.

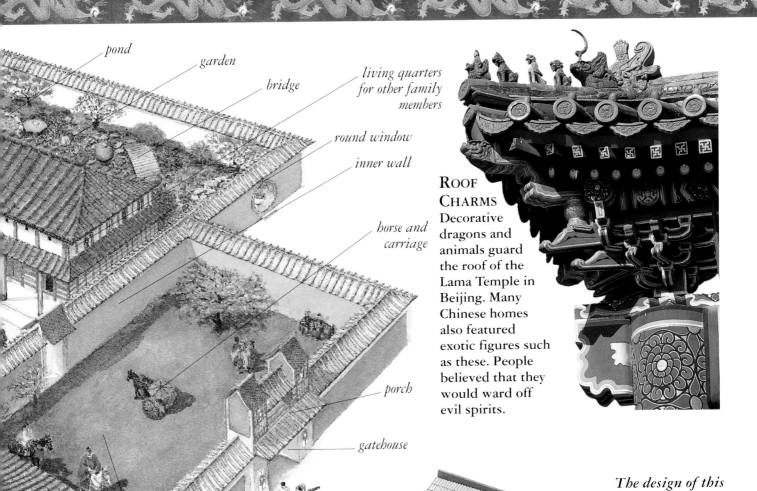

pond
garden
bridge
living quarters for other family members
round window
inner wall
horse and carriage
porch
gatehouse
outer wall
outer courtyard

ROOF CHARMS

Decorative dragons and animals guard the roof of the Lama Temple in Beijing. Many Chinese homes also featured exotic figures such as these. People believed that they would ward off evil spirits.

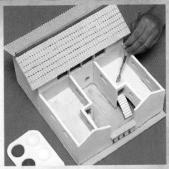

The design of this model is based on houses built in southern China. The overhanging roofs cover the courtyard. This helps to keep out rain, and provides shelter from the sun.

2 To assemble second side, repeat method described in step 1. If necessary, hold pieces together with masking tape while the glue dries.

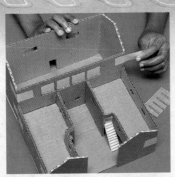

3 Glue B walls to the sides of the base, C wall to the back and D walls to the front. Hold with tape while glue dries. Glue gate between D walls.

4 Assemble A roofs (x2) and B roof (x1). Fix brackets underneath. Glue corrugated card (cut to same size as roof pieces), to top side of roofs.

5 Fix a small piece of card over the gate to make a porch. Paint house, as shown. Use a thin brush to create a tile effect on the removable roofs.

Traditional Life in China

T HE THINKER, CONFUCIUS (Kong Fuzi) lived from 551 B.C. to 479 B.C. He taught that just as the emperor was head of the state, the oldest man was head of the household and should be obeyed by his family. In reality, his wife often controlled the lives of everyone in the household.

During the Han dynasty (206 B.C.–A.D. 220), noblewomen were kept apart from the outside world. They could only gaze at the streets from the watchtowers of their homes. It was not until the Song dynasty (A.D. 960–1279) that they had more freedom. In poor households, women worked all day, spending long, tiring hours farming, cooking, sweeping, and washing.

For children of poor families, education meant learning to do the work their parents did. This involved carrying goods to market, and helping with the threshing and planting. Wealthier children had private tutors at home. Boys who hope to become scholars or civil servants learned to read and write Chinese characters. They also studied math and the works of Confucius.

LESSONS FOR THE BOYS
This group of Chinese boys have their school lessons. In imperial China, boys usually received a more academic education than girls. Girls were mainly taught music, handicrafts, painting, and social skills. Some girls were taught academic subjects, but they were not allowed to take the civil service tests.

FOOT BINDING
This foot looks elegant in its beautiful slipper, but it's a different story when the slipper is removed. Just when life was improving for Chinese women, the cruel new custom of footbinding was introduced. Dancers had bound their feet for some years in the belief that it made them look dainty. In the Song dynasty, the custom spread to wealthy and noble families. Little girls of five or so had their feet bound up so tightly that they became terribly deformed.

CHINESE MARRIAGE
A wedding ceremony takes place in the late 1800s. In imperial China, weddings were arranged by the parents of the bride and groom, rather than by the couples themselves. It was expected that the couple would respect their parents' wishes, even if they didn't like each other!

TAKING IT EASY

A noblewoman living from the Qing dynasty relaxes on a garden terrace with her children (c.1840). She is very fortunate, since she has little else to do but enjoy the pleasant surroundings of her home. In rich families like hers, servants did most of the hard work, such as cooking, cleaning, and washing. Wealthy Chinese families kept many servants, who usually lived in quarters inside their employer's home. Servants accounted for a large number of the workforce in imperial China. During the Ming dynasty (1368–1644), some 9,000 maidservants were employed at the imperial palace in Beijing alone!

RESPECT AND HONOUR

Children in the 1100s bow respectfully to their parents. Confucius taught that people should value and honor their families, including their ancestors. He believed that this helped to create a more orderly and virtuous society.

THE EMPEROR AND HIS MANY WIVES

Sui dynasty emperor Yangdi (A.D. 581–618) rides with his many womenfolk. Like many emperors, Yangdi was surrounded by women. An emperor married one woman, who would then become his empress, but he would still enjoy the company of concubines (secondary wives).

Food and Diet in China

Today, Chinese food is among the most popular in the world. Rice was the basis of most meals in ancient China, especially in the south, where it was grown. Northerners used wheat flour to make noodles and buns. Food varied greatly between the regions. The north was famous for pancakes, dumplings, lamb, and duck dishes. In the west, Sichuan was renowned for its hot chilli peppers. Mushrooms and bamboo shoots were popular along the lower Chang Jiang (Yangzi River).

For many people, meat was a rare treat. It included chicken, pork, and many kinds of fish, and was often spiced with garlic and ginger. Dishes featured meat that people from other parts of the world might find strange, such as turtle, dog, monkey and bear. Food was stewed, steamed, and fried. The use of chopsticks and bowls dates back to the Shang dynasty (*c.*1600–1122 B.C.).

THE KITCHEN GOD
A paper picture of the kitchen god and his wife hung in every kitchen. Each year, on the 24th day of the 12th month, sweets were put out as offerings. Then the picture was taken down and burned. A new one was hung in its place on New Year's Day.

A TANG BANQUET
In this picture, elegant ladies of the Tang court are sitting down to a feast. They are accompanied by music and singing, but there are no men present—women and men usually ate separately. This painting dates from the A.D. 900s, when raised tables came into fashion in China. Guests at banquets would wear their finest clothes. The most honored guest would sit to the east of the host, who sat facing south. The greatest honor of all was to be invited to dine with the emperor.

MAKE RED BEAN SOUP

You will need: measuring jug, food scale, measuring spoon, ¹/₂ lb. aduki beans, 3 tsp. ground nuts, 4 tsp. short-grain rice, cold water, tangerine, saucepan and lid, wooden spoon, ¹/₂ cup sugar, liquidizer, sieve, bowls.

1 Use the scale to weigh the aduki beans. Add the ground nuts and the short-grain rice. Measure 4 cups of cold water in the jug.

2 Wash and drain the beans and rice. Put them in a bowl. Add the cold water. Leave overnight to soak. Do not drain the water.

3 Wash and dry the tangerine. Then carefully remove the peel in a continuous strip. Leave the peel overnight, until it is hard and dry.

THAT SPECIAL TASTE

The Chinese flavor their food with a variety of herbs and spices. Garlic has been used in Chinese dishes and sauces for thousands of years. It may be chopped, crushed, pickled, or served whole. Root ginger is another crucial Chinese taste. Fresh chili peppers are used to make fiery dishes, and sesame provides flavoring in the form of paste, oil, and seeds.

sesame   *root ginger*

SHANG BRONZEWARE FIT FOR A FEAST

This three-legged bronze cooking pot dates from the Shang dynasty (*c.*1600 B.C.–1122 B.C.). Its green appearance is caused by the reaction of the metal to air over the 3,500 years since it was made. During Shang rule, metalworkers made many vessels out of bronze, including cooking pots and wine jars. They were used in all kinds of ceremonies, and at feasts people held in honor of their dead ancestors.

BUTCHERS AT WORK

The stone carving (*right*) shows farmers butchering cattle in about A.D. 50. In early China, cooks would cut up meat with square-shaped cleavers. It was flavored with wines and spices, and simmered in big pots over open fires until it was tender.

Most peasant farmers lived on a simple diet. Red bean soup with rice was a typical daily meal. Herbs and spices were often added to make the food taste more interesting.

4 Put the soaked beans and rice (plus the soaking liquid) into a large saucepan. Add the dried tangerine peel and 2 cups of cold water.

5 Bring the mixture to boiling point. Reduce the heat, cover the saucepan, and simmer for 2 hours. Stir occasionally. If the liquid boils away, add more water.

6 When the beans are just covered with the water, add the sugar. Simmer this until the sugar has completely dissolved.

7 Remove and discard the tangerine peel. Leave soup to cool, uncovered. Puree the soup. Strain any lumps with a sieve. Pour into bowls.

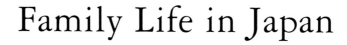

Family Life in Japan

FAMILIES IN EARLY JAPAN survived by working together in the family business or on the family land. Japanese people believed that the family group was more important than any one individual. Family members were supposed to consider the wellbeing of the whole family first, before thinking about their own needs and plans. Sometimes, this led to quarrels or disappointments. For example, younger brothers in poor families were often not allowed to marry, so that the family land could be handed on, undivided, to the eldest son. Daughters would leave home to marry if a suitable husband could be found. If not, they also remained single and stayed in their parents' house.

Family responsibility passed down the generations, from father to eldest son. Japanese families respected age and experience, because they believed it brought wisdom.

BRINGING UP BABY

It was women's work to care for young children. This painting shows an elegant young mother from a rich family dressing her son in a kimono (a robe with wide sleeves). The family maid holds the belt for the boy's kimono, and a pet cat watches nearby.

WORK

A little boy uses a simple machine to help winnow rice. (Winnowing separates the edible grains of rice from the outer husks.) Boys and girls from farming families were expected to help with work around the house and farmyard, and in the fields.

CARP STREAMER

You will need: pencil, 2 large sheets of paper, felt-tip pen, scissors, paints, paintbrush, water pot, glue, wire, masking tape, string, piece of cane.

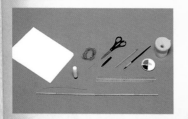

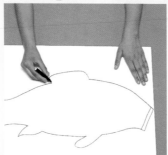

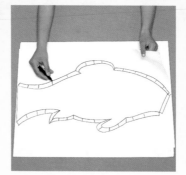

1 Take the pencil and one piece of paper. Draw a large carp fish shape on the paper. When you are happy with the shape, go over it in felt-tip pen.

2 Put the second piece of paper over the first. Draw around the fish shape. Next, draw a border around the second fish, and add tabs, as shown.

3 Add scales, eyes, fins, and other details to both of the fishes, as shown above. Cut them both out, remembering to snip into the tabs. Paint both fishes.

PLAYTIME

These young boys have started two tops spinning close to each other. They are waiting to see what will happen when the tops touch. Japanese children had many different toys with which to play. In addition to the spinning top, another big favorite was the kite.

TRADITIONAL MEDICINE

Kuzu (Japanese arrowroot) and ginger are ingredients that have been used for centuries as treatments in traditional Japanese medicine. Most traditional drugs are made from vegetables. The kuzu and ginger are mixed together in different ways, depending on the symptoms of the patient. For example, there are 20 different mixtures for treating colds. Ginger is usually used when there is no fever.

kuzu   *ginger*

HONORING ANCESTORS

A mother, father, and child make offerings and say their prayers at a small family altar in their house. The lighted candle and paper lantern help guide the spirits to their home. Families honored their dead ancestors at special festivals. At the festival of Obon, in the summer, they greeted family spirits who had returned to earth.

4 Put the two fish shapes together, with the painted sides out. Turn the tabs in and glue the edges of the fish together, except for the tail and the mouth.

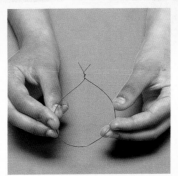

5 Use garden wire to make a ring the size of the mouth. Twist the ends together, then bend them back. Wrap masking tape around the ends.

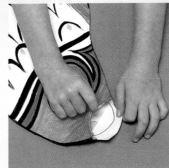

6 Place the ring in the fish's mouth. Glue the ends of the mouth over the ring. Tie one end of some string on to the mouth ring, and the other end to a garden cane.

Families fly carp streamers on Boy's Day (the fifth day of the fifth month) every year. One carp is flown for each son. Carp are symbols of perseverance and strength.

Growing Up in Greece

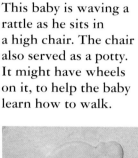

CHILDREN IN EARLY TIMES faced many obstacles as they grew up. In ancient Greece, when a baby was born, its father would decide whether to keep or abandon it. A sick or handicapped baby might be left outdoors at birth. Whoever rescued the child could raise it as their slave. Girls were more likely to be rejected because they could not provide for their parents in adulthood. Many children died in infancy due to poor healthcare.

Education was considered to be important for boys. Even so, it was usually only sons in rich families who received a complete schooling. They were taught a variety of subjects, including reading, music and gymnastics. Boys from poor families often learned their father's trade. Education in domestic skills was essential for most girls. A notable exception was in Sparta, where the girls joined boys in hard physical training.

BABY STEPS
This baby is waving a rattle as he sits in a high chair. The chair also served as a potty. It might have wheels on it, to help the baby learn how to walk.

BULLY OFF
These two boys are playing a game similar to hockey. In general, team sports were ignored in favor of sports activities where an individual could excel. Wrestling and athletics are two such examples. They were encouraged as training for war.

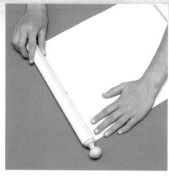

YOU ARE IT
Two girls play a kind of ta game, in which the loser has to carry the winner. Girls had less free time than boys did. They were supposed to stay close to home and help their mothers with housework, cooking, and taking care of the younger children.

MAKE A SCROLL
You will need: 2 x 1 ft. rods of balsa wood, 2 in. in diameter, 4 doorknobs, double-sided sticky tape, sheet of paper 1 x 1 ft., 1 x 2 ³/₄ in. rod of balsa wood, ³/₄ in. in diameter, craft knife, paintbrush, white glue, ink powder.

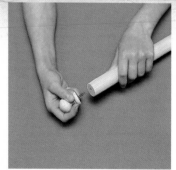

1 Carefully screw a door knob into both ends of each 1-foot rod of balsa wood, or ask an adult to do it for you. These are the end pieces of the scroll.

2 Cut two pieces of double-sided tape 12 inches long. Stick one piece of tape along the top of the paper and another along the bottom.

3 Wrap the top of the paper once around one of the pieces of balsa wood. Repeat this step again for the second piece at the bottom of the paper.

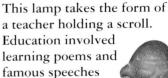

ACTION DOLL

The arms and legs on this terra-cotta figure are attached with cord, so that the shoulders and knees can be moved. A doll such as this was a luxury item, which only a wealthy family could afford to buy for its children. Other popular toys were rattles and hoops.

LIGHT OF LEARNING

This lamp takes the form of a teacher holding a scroll. Education involved learning poems and famous speeches from scrolls by heart. This was thought to help boys make effective speeches in court and at public meetings. Good orators were always admired, and could wield much influence.

THE ALPHABET

The first two of the Greek alphabet's 24 letters are called alpha and beta—these names give us the English word "alphabet."

ΑΒΓΔΕΖΗΘΙ
A B G D E Z e TH I

ΚΛΜΝΞΟΠΡΣ
K L M N X O P R S

ΤΥΦΧΨΩ
T U PH KH PS o

Scrolls in ancient Greece were usually made from animal skin.

A SECOND MOTHER

Greeks often hired wet nurses (*on the left*) to breastfeed their babies. Some nurses were forbidden to drink wine, in case it affected their milk, or made them so drunk that they might harm the baby.

ΑΧΙΛΛΕΥΣ

4 Ask an adult to help you with this step. Take the 2 3/4 piece of balsa wood, and use your craft knife to sharpen the end of it into a point.

5 Paint the tip of your pen with glue. This will stop the wood from soaking up the ink. Add water to the ink powder to make ink.

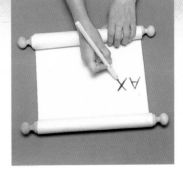

6 Write some letters or a word on your scroll with your pen. We've translated the Greek alphabet above in the fact box. Use this as a guide.

7 We have copied some letters in ancient Greek. You could also write a word. Ask a friend to translate what you have written using the alphabet.

Roman Houses

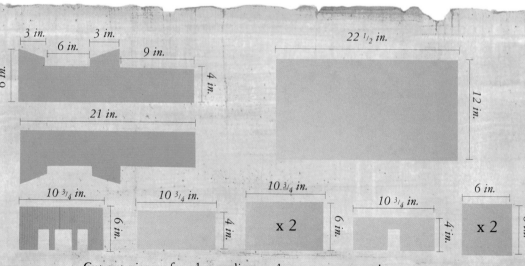

garden

bedroom

tablinium
(living room
and office)

During the Roman Era, wealthy citizens could afford to live in their own private house. A typical town house was designed to look inward, with the rooms arranged around a central courtyard and a walled garden. Outside walls had few windows, and these were small and shuttered. The front door opened onto a short passage that led into an airy courtyard called an atrium. Front rooms on either side of the passage were usually used as bedrooms. Sometimes they were used as workshops or shops, and they had shutters that opened to the street. The middle of the atrium was open to the sky. Below this opening was a pool, set into the floor, to collect rainwater. Around the atrium were more bedrooms and the kitchen. If you were a guest or had important business, you would be shown into the tablinium. The dining room, or triclinium, was often the grandest room of all. Very rich people also had a summer dining room overlooking the garden. Houses were made of local building materials. These might include stone, mud bricks, cement, and timber. Roofs were made of clay tiles.

LOCKS AND KEYS
This was the key to the door of a Roman house. Pushed in through a keyhole, the prongs at the end of the key fitted into holes in the bolt in the lock. The key could then be used to slide the bolt along and unlock the door.

INSIDE A ROMAN HOME
The outside of a wealthy Roman's town house was usually very plain, but inside it was highly decorated with elaborate wall paintings and intricate mosaics. The rooms were sparsely furnished, with couches and beds, small side tables, benches, and folding stools. There were few windows, but high ceilings and wide doors made the most of the light from the open atrium and the garden.

MAKE A ROMAN HOME
You will need: pencil, ruler, thick card, scissors, white glue, paintbrushes, masking tape, corrugated cardboard, thin card, water pot, acrylic paints.

3 in.   3 in.
6 in.   9 in.

6 in.

4 in.

21 in.

22 ½ in.

12 in.

10 ¾ in.   10 ¾ in.   10 ¾ in.   10 ¾ in.   6 in.

6 in.   4 in.   x 2   6 in.   4 in.   x 2   6 in.

Cut out pieces of card according to the measurements shown.

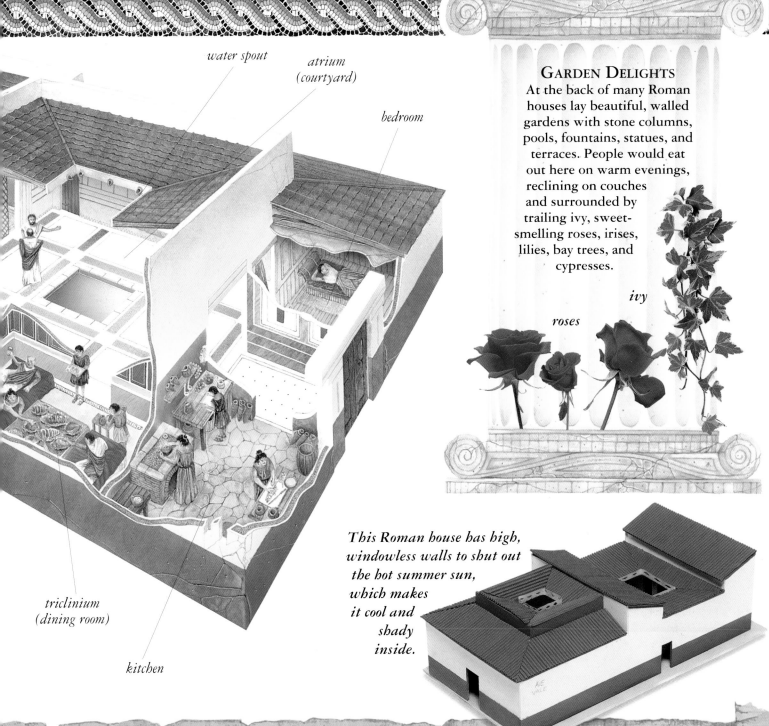

water spout

atrium
(courtyard)

bedroom

triclinium
(dining room)

kitchen

GARDEN DELIGHTS

At the back of many Roman houses lay beautiful, walled gardens with stone columns, pools, fountains, statues, and terraces. People would eat out here on warm evenings, reclining on couches and surrounded by trailing ivy, sweet-smelling roses, irises, lilies, bay trees, and cypresses.

ivy

roses

This Roman house has high, windowless walls to shut out the hot summer sun, which makes it cool and shady inside.

1 Cut out the pieces of thick card. Edge each piece with glue. Press the pieces together, and reinforce with masking tape. You have now made the walls of your house.

2 Measure your model and cut out pieces of corrugated cardboard for the roofs. Stick them together with glue, as shown above. Paint the roofs red.

3 Rainwater running down the sloped atrium roof was directed into a pool below by gutters and water spouts. Make gutters from strips of thin card, with holes as spouts.

4 Paint the house walls as shown, using masking tape to get a straight line. Glue on the roofs. Why not finish off your Roman house with some authentic graffiti!

Family Occasions in Rome

This Roman tombstone from Germany shows a family gathered together for a meal. From the Latin inscription on it, we know that it was put up by a soldier of the legions, in memory of his dead wife. He lovingly describes her as the "sweetest and purest" of women.

T HE FAMILY was very important to Romans. The father was the all-powerful head of the family, which included everyone in the household—the wife, children, slaves, and even close relatives. In the early days of Rome, a father had the power of life and death over his children! However, Roman fathers were rarely harsh, and children were much loved by both parents.

Childhood was fairly short. Parents would arrange for a girl to be betrothed at the age of 12, and a boy at 14. Marriages took place a few years later. Brides usually wore a white dress and a yellow cloak, with an orange veil and a wreath of sweetly scented flowers. A sacrifice would be made to the gods, and everyone would wish the couple well. That evening, a procession with flaming torches and flute music would lead the newly weds to their home.

Funerals were also marked with music and processions. By Roman law, burials and cremations had to take place outside the city walls.

MOTHER AND BABY

A mother tends to her baby in the cradle. When children were born, they were laid at the feet of their father. If he accepted the child, he would pick it up. In wealthy families, a birth was a great joy, but for poorer families it just meant another mouth to feed. Romans named a girl on the eighth day after the birth, and a boy on the ninth day. The child was given a bulla, a charm to ward off evil spirits.

TOGETHERNESS

When a couple were engaged, they would exchange gifts as a symbol of their devotion to each other. A ring like this one might have been given by a man to his future bride. The clasped hands symbolize marriage. Gold pendants with similar patterns were also popular.

MOURNING THE DEAD

A wealthy Roman has died and his family have gone into mourning. Laments are played on flutes as they prepare his body for the funeral procession. The Romans believed that the dead went to Hades, the Underworld, which lay beyond the river of the dead. A coin was placed in the corpse's mouth, to pay the ferryman. Food and drinks for the journey were buried with the body.

TILL DEATH US DO PART

A Roman marriage ceremony was much like a present-day Christian wedding. The couple would exchange vows and clasp hands to symbolize their union. Here, the groom is holding the marriage contract, which would have been drawn up before the ceremony. Not everyone found happiness, however, and divorce was very common.

WEDDING FLOWERS

Roman brides wore a veil on their wedding day. This was often crowned with a wreath of flowers. In the early days of the Empire, verbena and sweet marjoram were a popular combination. Later fashions included orange blossom and myrtle, whose fragrant flowers were sacred to Venus, the goddess of love.

orange blossom

verbena

Roman Education

MOST CHILDREN in the Roman Empire never went to school. They either learned a trade from their parents, or studied math by trading on a market stall. Boys might be trained to fight with swords and to ride horses, in preparation for joining the army. Girls would be taught how to run the home, in preparation for marriage.

Wealthy families did provide an education for their sons, and sometimes for their daughters, too. They were usually taught at home by a private tutor, but there were also small schools. Tutors and teachers would teach children arithmetic, and how to read and write both Latin and Greek. Intelligent pupils might also learn public speaking skills, poetry, and history. Girls often had music lessons at home, on a harp-like instrument called a lyre.

INKPOTS AND PENS

A pen and ink were used to write on scrolls made from papyrus (a kind of reed) or thin sheets of wood. Ink was often made from soot or lamp-black, mixed with water. It was kept in inkpots such as these. Inkpots were made from glass, pottery, and metal. Pens were made from bone, reeds, and bronze.

WRITING IN WAX

This painting shows a couple from Pompeii. The man holds a parchment scroll. His wife is probably going through their household accounts. She holds a wax-covered writing tablet and a stylus, to scratch words into the wax. A stylus had a pointed end for writing and a flat end for erasing.

A WRITING TABLET

You will need: sheets and sticks of balsa wood, craft knife, ruler, white glue, paintbrush, brown acrylic paint, water pot, modeling clay, work board, rolling pin, modeling tool, skewer, purple thread, pencil (to be used as a stylus), gold paint.

1 Use the craft knife to cut the balsa sheet into two rectangles, 4 x 8 ¾ in. The sticks of balsa should be cut into four pieces 8 ¾ in. long, and four pieces 4 in. long.

2 Glue the sticks around the edges of each sheet as shown. These form a shallow hollow into which you can press the "wax." Paint the two frames a rich brown color.

3 Roll the modeling clay on a board, and place a balsa frame on top. Use the modeling tool to cut around the outside of the frame. Repeat this step.

TEACHER AND PUPILS

A stone sculpture from Roman Germany shows a teacher seated between two of his pupils. They are reading their lessons from papyrus scrolls. Children had to learn poetry and other writings by heart. Any bad behavior or mistakes were punished with a beating.

WRITING IT DOWN

Various materials were used for writing. Melted beeswax was poured into wooden trays to make writing tablets. Letters were scratched into the wax, which could be used again and again. Powdered soot was mixed with water to make ink for writing on papyrus, parchment, and wood.

soot

melted beeswax

Roman numerals on papyrus

I	II	III	IV	V
1	2	3	4	5
VI	VII	VIII	IX	X
6	7	8	9	10

LETTERS IN STONE

Temples, monuments, and public buildings were covered in Latin inscriptions, such as this one. Each letter was beautifully chiseled by a stonemason. These words are carved in marble. The inscription marked the 14th birthday of Lucius Caesar, the grandson of the Emperor Augustus.

4 Cut off about ¹/₂ in. all around the edge of each modeling clay rectangle. This helps to make sure that the modeling clay will fit inside the balsa wood frame.

5 Carefully press the clay into each side—this represents the wax. Use the skewer to poke two holes through the inside edge of each frame, as shown.

6 Connect the two frames by threading purple thread through each pair of holes, and tying it securely together. You have now made your tablet.

Paint the pencil gold to make it look like it is made from metal. Use it like a stylus to scratch words on your tablet. Why not try writing in Latin? You could write CIVIS ROMANVS SVM, which means, "I am a Roman citizen."

Celtic Food and Drink

FOOD WAS VERY IMPORTANT TO THE CELTS. They enjoyed eating and drinking, and were not ashamed of getting drunk, or of rowdy behavior. They did not, however, approve of people getting too fat. Roman writers reported that Celtic warriors were ordered not to let out their belts, but to lose weight, when clothes around their waists became too tight! The Celts produced most of their own food on their farms. They needed to buy only items such as salt (used to preserve meat and fish), and luxury goods such as wine. They also hunted and fished for many wild creatures, and gathered wild fruits, nuts, herbs, and mushrooms from meadows and forests. Celtic families were famous throughout Europe for their hospitality to strangers. It was their custom to offer food and drinks to any visitor, and not to ask who they were or where they were from until the end of the meal.

HANGING CAULDRON
Meals for large numbers of people were cooked in a big cauldron. This bronze cauldron, iron chain and hook were made around 300 B.C. in Switzerland. A cauldron could also be used for boiling water, heating milk to make cheese, and brewing mead.

CELTIC CASSEROLE
Meat, beans, grains, and herbs were stewed in a covered clay pot. The pot could be placed directly on glowing embers, or (as shown here) balanced on a hearthstone. This stone hearth, with a hollow pit for the fire, was found at an oppidum (Celtic town) in France.

MAKE SOME OATCAKES
You will need: 2 cups oatmeal, ²/₃ cup flour, salt, baking soda, ¹/₂ stick butter, water, bowl, sifter, wooden spoon, small saucepan, heat-resistant glass, board, rolling pin, baking tray, wire rack.

1 Preheat the oven to 425°F. Put 2 cups of oatmeal into a large bowl. Add the flour and sift it into the bowl, with the oatmeal.

2 Next add 1 teaspoon of salt to the oatmeal and flour mix. Mix all the ingredients in the bowl together thoroughly, using a wooden spoon.

3 Add a quarter teaspoon of baking soda to the oatmeal and flour. Mix together thoroughly, and then put the bowl to one side.

GRINDING GRAIN

All kinds of grain were ground into flour using hand-powered querns (mills) like this one. The grains were poured through a hole in the top stone. This stone was turned around and around. The grains became trapped and were crushed between the top and bottom stones, then spilled out of the quern sides as flour.

FRUITS FROM THE FOREST

The Celts liked eating many of the same fruits and nuts that we enjoy today. However, they had to go and find them growing on bushes and trees. We know that the Celts ate fruit, because archaeologists have found many seeds and stones on garbage heaps and in lavatory pits at Celtic sites.

wild cherries

apples

hazelnuts

blackberries

OUT HUNTING

Celtic men hunted and fished for sport, and also as a way of finding food. This stone carving, which shows a huntsman and his dogs chasing deer, was made around A.D. 800 in Scotland. By then, Celtic power had declined, but many traditions persisted.

Enjoy your oatcakes plain, like the Celts did, or eat them with butter, cheese, or honey. All these were favorite Celtic foods. Today, some people put jam on their oatcakes, but sugar (used to make jam) was unknown in Europe in Celtic times.

4 Next, melt the butter in a small saucepan over low heat. Make sure that it does not burn. Add the melted butter to the oats and flour.

5 Boil some water. Put a little water in a mug or heat-resistant glass. Gradually add the boiled water to the mix, enough to make a stiff dough.

6 Turn the dough out on a board sprinkled with a little oatmeal and flour. Roll the dough until it is about $1/2$ in. thick. Cut the dough into 24 circles.

7 Put the circles of dough on a greased baking tray. Bake in the oven for 15 minutes. Allow the oatcakes to cool on a wire rack before serving.

Viking Family Life

IN EARLY TIMES, everybody in the family knew who was related to whom, and where they lived. For the Vikings, even distant relatives played an important role in the family, in addition to grandparents, aunts, and uncles. They were all very aware of family links, and loyalty was fierce. If one member of a family was harmed, then the other members of the family would seek revenge. This led to feuds—quarrels between one family and another—that simmered from one generation to the next. Feuds could lead to fights, burglaries, and sometimes even murder.

The father of the household had great power over other members of the family. If he thought a newborn baby was a weakling, he could leave it to die. When a Viking farmer died, his eldest son inherited the farm. The rest of the family would have to move away, and the younger sons had to find new land of their own to farm. Mothers were often strong, determined women who had great influence in the family. There was little schooling. Learning how to fight with a sword or use an ax was more important than reading and writing. As children grew up, they were expected to work hard and to help around the house. They were sometimes fostered by families on other farms and had to work in return for their keep.

HELPING OUT
This reconstruction of a market stall in Jorvik shows a young boy helping his parents during a day's trading. Children often followed in the same trade as their parents. This boy would have learned how to haggle over prices. He would also know how to weigh silver.

FAMILY MEMORIALS
The Vikings often put up memorial stones to honor relatives and friends when they died. This stone from Sweden was put up by Tjagan and Gunnar in loving memory of their brother Vader.

LIVING IN FEAR

Old tales tell how Vikings fought each other mercilessly during long, bitter feuds between families. Murderous bands might turn up at a longhouse by night, threatening to burn down the roof and kill everybody inside. Viking households also risked attack from local peoples and other raiders wherever they settled.

WANTING CHILDREN

A woman who wanted to make a good marriage and have children would pray to Frey, the god of love and fertility. On these gold foil charms from Sweden, Frey is shown with his beautiful wife Gerda. She was the daughter of a giant called Gymir.

GROWING UP

Children were expected to work hard in Viking times. Boys were taught farming, rowing, and sailing. Girls were taught how to spin and weave, milk cows, and prepare food. When all the daily tasks had been done, boys probably played games or went fishing. Viking girls may have spent some of their free time gathering berries and mushrooms.

BURIAL GRAVE

This skeleton belongs to a Viking woman from Iceland. Archaeologists have been able to tell how women lived in the Viking age by examining the goods placed in their graves. These were possessions for them to use in the next world.

Viking Women

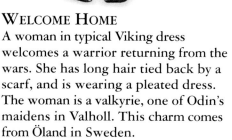

WOMEN WERE not allowed to speak in Viking public assemblies, where laws and judgements were passed, yet they had more independence than many European women at the time. They could choose their own husband, own property, and be granted a divorce. At a wedding, both the bride and groom had to make their marriage vows before witnesses. Memorial stones show that many husbands loved their wives and treated them with respect.

It was the women who usually managed the farm while their men were off raiding or trading. They never knew if their husbands, brothers, and sons would return from their travels or be lost in a storm at sea. Women certainly needed to be tough in the harsh landscapes and cold climates of countries such as Iceland and Greenland. It was their job to make woolen or linen clothes for the family, to prepare and cook food, and to clean the home.

WELCOME HOME
A woman in typical Viking dress welcomes a warrior returning from the wars. She has long hair tied back by a scarf, and is wearing a pleated dress. The woman is a valkyrie, one of Odin's maidens in Valholl. This charm comes from Öland in Sweden.

A DAY'S WORK
In this reconstruction from Jorvik (York, England), a Viking woman goes out to fetch water from the well. Hissing geese beat their wings and scatter in her path. Women's work lasted from dawn until nightfall, with clothes to darn, poultry to tend, meals to cook, and children to scold! Most women also spent several hours a day spinning and weaving wool into cloth to make clothes.

PRACTICAL BUT PRETTY

Viking women wore long tunics fastened by a pair of brooches. This Viking brooch was found in Denmark. It is over 1,000 years old, and is made of gold. Women wore clothing that was both practical and comfortable.

GETTING READY

Before a wedding or a visit to the fair, a Viking woman may have smoothed or pleated her dress on a board like this one. A glass ball would have been used instead of an iron. This whalebone board comes from Norway.

WEAVING AT HOME

Viking looms were much like this one. The warps, or upright threads, hang from a crossbar. The weft, or cross threads, pass between them to make cloth. Weaving was done by women in every Viking home.

THE NEW QUEEN

In this picture, Queen Aelfgyfu is shown alongside her husband King Cnut, in England. Aelfgyfu was Cnut's second wife. They are placing a cross on an altar. Queens were the most powerful women in Scandinavian society.

BELOVED WIFE

This stone was put up by King Gorm as a monument to his wife. The inscription reads "King Gorm made this memorial to his wife Thyri, adornment of Denmark." The messages written on such stones show the qualities that Vikings admired most in women.

North American Homes

Native American peoples built houses that were cleverly adapted to their surroundings. During the winter months, the Inuit of the far north built dome-shaped homes out of blocks of ice or with hard soil, wood, and whale bones. Where wood was plentiful, such as in the eastern part of the United States, people built a variety of homes. The wikiup, or wigwam, was dome shaped and made out of thatch, bark, or hide, which was tightly woven across an arch of bent branches. Basic, rectangular thatched houses were built from a construction of chopped twigs covered with a mix of clay and straw, or mud. Near the East Coast, massive longhouses, up to 150 feet long, with barrel-shaped roofs, were made from local trees. Some tribes lived in different kinds of shelters depending on the season. The Plains nations lived mostly in tipis (hide tents) and earth lodges. The nearest to modern buildings were the homes of the Pueblos in the Southwest. These were terraced, mud brick villages. Pueblos also built round underground ceremonial chambers with hidden entrances in the roof.

AT HOME
A Mandan chief relaxes with his family and dogs inside his lodge. Notice how a hole is cut in the roof, to let out smoke from the fire and let fresh air in. Earth lodges were popular with Mandan and Hidatsa people on the Upper Missouri. The layout followed strict customs. The family would sleep on the south side; guests slept on the north. Stores and weapons were stored at the back. The owner of this home has his horse inside, to prevent it from being stolen when the family is asleep.

HOMES ON THE PLAINS
The hides of around 12 buffaloes were used to cover a family tipi that belonged to a Plains family. "Tipi" comes from a Siouan word meaning "to dwell." Hides were sewn together and stretched over wooden poles about 25 feet high. When it became too hot inside, the tipi sides were rolled up. In the winter, a fire was lit in the center.

TOTEM POLE
Totem poles were usually found in the northwestern corner of the United States. They were carved out of wood, often from the mighty red cedar (thuja) trees. Tall totem poles were erected outside the long plank houses of the Haida people. These homes were shared by several families. The poles were carved and painted to keep a record of the family histories of the people inside. They were also sometimes made to honor a great chief.

EARTH LODGES

Mandan people perform the Buffalo Dance in front of their lodges. These were built with logs to create a dome frame, which was then covered over with tightly packed earth.

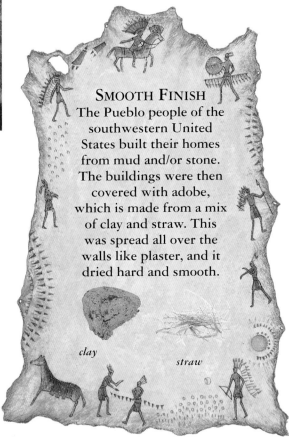

SMOOTH FINISH

The Pueblo people of the southwestern United States built their homes from mud and/or stone. The buildings were then covered with adobe, which is made from a mix of clay and straw. This was spread all over the walls like plaster, and it dried hard and smooth.

clay

straw

LAYERS OF BRICK

This ruin was once part of a complex of Pueblo buildings. Pueblo homes were often multistoried with flat roofs. The floors were reached by ladders. Circular brick chambers were built underground. These were the kivas used for religious and ceremonial rites.

les in the
of let
t smoke

sleeping platform

higher platform
for storing food

groups of longhouses
were built together,
sometimes inside a
protective fence.

THE LONGHOUSE

The Iroquois people of the Woodlands built long wooden houses. The frames were made of poles hewn from tree trunks, with cladding made from sheets of thick bark. Homes were communal. Many families lived in one longhouse, each with their own section built around an open fire.

Tribal Family Roles

ROLES WITHIN THE TRIBAL NORTH AMERICAN FAMILY were well defined. The men were the hunters, protectors, and leaders. Women tended the crops, made clothes, cared for the home and the sick, and prepared the food. The children's early days were carefree, but they quickly learned to respect their elders. From an early age, young girls were taught the skills of craftwork and homemaking by their mothers, and the boys learned to use weapons and hunt from the men. Girls as young as 12 years old could be married. Boys had to exchange presents with their future in-laws before the marriage was allowed to take place. At birth, most children were named by a grandparent. Later, as adults, they could choose another name of their own.

BONES FOR DINNER
This spoon was carved from animal bone. For the early family, there were no metal utensils. Many items were made from bone, tusks, antlers, and horns. Bone was also used to make bowls.

HOLDING THE BABY
A woman holds her baby strapped to a cradleboard. Domestic scenes were often the focus of crafts, which reflected the importance of family life.

A DAY'S HUNTING
Blackfoot girls watch as men leave camp on a hunting trip. They are in search of bison. If the hunt is successful, the women will help skin the animals, then stretch out the hides to dry. Buffalo skins were used to make tipi covers. Softer buckskin, from deer, was used for clothing.

MAKE A KACHINA DOLL

You will need: cardboard roll, ruler, scissors, compass, pencil, thick card, white glue, brush for glue, masking tape, paints in cream/yellow, green/blue red and black, paintbrush, water pot, red paper.

1 Take the cardboard roll and cut a section of about a third off of the top. This will form the head piece. The larger end will form the body.

2 Use the compass (or end of the cardboard roll) to draw four circles about 1-in. radius on card. Then draw a smaller circle $3/4$ in. radius. Cut them all out.

3 Glue the larger circles to both ends of both of the cardboard roll tubes. Allow to dry. Glue the smaller circle of card on top of one end of the longer roll.

ROLE PLAY

Children love to copy their elders, and this little Sioux girl is wearing an adult's large headdress. She is holding a favorite doll to pose for the picture. Playing with dolls taught girls about their future role as carers. Boys enjoyed learning how to ride, shoot arrows, and hunt.

FAMILY GATHERING

A family from the Cree nation in Canada enjoys a quiet evening around the fire. Native American families were usually small, since no more than two or three children survived the harsh life. However, a lodge was often home to an extended family. There could be two or three sisters, their families, and grandparents under one roof.

Kachina dolls were made by the Hopi people to represent different spirits. This is the Corn kachina. Some parents gave the dolls to their children to help them learn about tribal customs.

BABY CARRIER

For the first year of its life, a baby would spend its time strapped to a cradleboard, such as this one inspired by the eastern Woodland tribes. It was also used by eastern Sioux, Iowa, Pawnee, and Osage parents. A baby could sleep or be carried in safety in its cradle, leaving the mother free to work. The board was strapped to the mother's back.

4 The smaller cardboard circle forms the doll's neck. Glue the small cardboard roll (the head) on top of the larger cardboard roll (the body).

5 Cut two small L-shapes from card to form the arms. Then cut two small ear shapes from the card. Cover these shapes with masking tape.

6 Glue the arms to the body, and the ears to the sides of the head, so that they stick out at right angles. Paint the doll the colors shown above.

7 While the paint is drying, cut two small feather shapes from red paper. Glue these to the top of the doll's head, so that they stick into the air.

Cold-Climate Homes

MOST ANCIENT ARCTIC GROUPS lived in small villages that contained a few families at most. The villages were spread out over a wide area, so each group had a large territory in which to hunt. In the winter, the Inuit, Saami, and other arctic tribes lived in sturdy houses that were built partly underground to protect them from the freezing conditions above. In the summer, or when they traveled from place to place, they lived in tents or temporary shelters.

In Siberia and parts of Scandinavia, groups such as the Nenets did not settle in one place. Their homes were lightweight tents—called chums in Siberia—which were frameworks made from wooden poles, covered with animal skins. Chums could withstand severe arctic blizzards, and kept

TENT LIFE
A Nenet herder loads a sled outside his family's chum in preparation for another day's travel across Siberia. Chums were convenient, light, and easy to assemble and dismantle. Some Nenets still live in chums, as their ancestors have done for many generations.

BUILDING MATERIALS
A deserted building made from stone and whale bone stands on a cliff in Siberia. Building materials were scarce in the Arctic. In coastal regions, people built houses with whale bones and driftwood gathered from the beach. Inland, houses were mainly built with rocks and turf.

ARCTIC DWELLING
This illustration shows a house in subarctic Alaska, with a section removed to show how it is made. Houses such as this one were buried under the ground. People entered by ladder through the roof.

MAKE A NENET TENT
You will need: 3 blankets (two 6½ x 5 ft. and one 4 x 4 ft.), tape measure, string, scissors, 10 bamboo sticks (nine 5 ft. long and one 1 ft. long), black marker pen, black thread, a log or a stone.

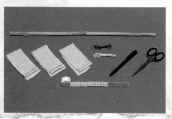

1 Cut small holes 4 in. apart along the shorter sides of the two large blankets. Thread a piece of string through the holes, and tie the string together.

2 Cut a 1 ft. 10 in. piece of string. Tie the 1-ft.-long stick and a black marker 22 in. apart. Use the marker to draw a circle on the smaller blanket.

3 Tie four bamboo sticks together at one end. Open out the sticks on the base blanket. Put the sticks on the edge of the circle so they stand up.

BONY BUNKER
Whale bone rafters arch over the remains of a home in Siberia. Part of the house was often built underground. First, the builders dug a pit to make the floor. Then they built low walls of rocks and turf. Long bones or driftwood laid on top of the walls formed sturdy rafters that supported a roof made from turf and stones.

MAKING WINDOWS
An old stone and turf house stands in arctic Greenland. Ancient peoples made windows by stretching a dried seal bladder over a hole in the wall. The bladder was thin enough to let light through.

A tent covered with several layers of animal skins made an extremely warm arctic home, even in the bitterly cold winter. The wooden poles were lashed together with rope.

4 Lean the five extra bamboo sticks against the main frame, placing the ends around the base circle. Leave a gap at the front for the entrance.

5 Tie the middle of the edge of the two larger blankets to the back of the frame, at the top. Make two tight knots to secure the blankets.

6 Bring each blanket around to the entrance. Tie them at the top with string. Roll the blankets down to the base, so that they lie flat on the frame.

7 Tie five 40 in. pieces of thread along the front edge of the blanket. Pull these tight, and tie to a log or stone to weigh down the base of the tent.

Arctic Seasonal Camps

CHEERFUL GLOW
An igloo near Thule, Greenland, is lit up by a primus stove. The light inside reveals the spiraling shape of the blocks of ice used to make the igloo. Snow crystals in the walls scatter the light, and the whole room is bathed in the glow. In the Inuit language, "iglu" is actually a word to describe any type of house. A shelter such as this one is called an igluigaq.

SUMMER IS A BUSY TIME for arctic animals and plants. The lives of arctic peoples changed with the seasons, too. The rising temperature melts the sea ice, and the oceans teem with tiny organisms called plankton. On land, the tundra explodes into flower. Insects hatch and burrowing creatures, such as lemmings, leave their tunnels in search of food. Wild reindeer, whales, and many types of birds migrate to the Arctic to feast on the plentiful supply of food.

In Canada, Alaska, and Greenland, the Inuit left their winter villages and traveled to the summer hunting grounds. They hunted fish and sea mammals, and gathered fruits and berries, taking advantage of the long, bright summer days.

During winter hunting trips, the Inuit built temporary shelters made of snow blocks, commonly called igloos. The basic igloo design was developed hundreds of years ago. It kept the hunters warm, even in the harshest arctic storm.

BUILDING AN IGLOO
An Inuk (an Inuit man) builds an igloo, using a long ice knife to cut large blocks of tightly packed snow. First, he lays a ring of ice blocks to make a circle up to $3\frac{1}{2}$ yards in diameter. Then, some of the blocks are cut to make them slope. As new blocks are added, the walls of the igloo begin to lean inward, forming a dome-shaped igloo. This method is exactly the same as the one used by his ancestors centuries ago.

MAKE A MODEL IGLOO
You will need: self-drying clay, rolling pin, cutting board, ruler, modeling tool, scissors, thick card (8 x 8 in.), pencil, water bowl, white paint, paint brush.

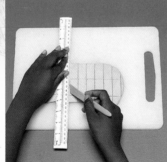

1 Roll out the self-drying clay. It should be around $\frac{3}{8}$-in. thick. Cut out 30 blocks of clay; 24 must be $\frac{3}{4}$ x $1\frac{1}{2}$ in., and the other 6 must be $\frac{1}{2}$ x $\frac{3}{4}$ in.

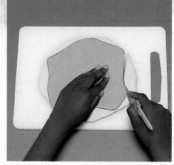

2 Cut out some card to make an irregular shape. Roll out more clay. Put the template on the clay, and cut around it to make the base of the igloo.

3 Mark a circle with a diameter of $4\frac{3}{4}$ in. Cut out a small rectangle on the edge of the circle ($\frac{3}{4}$ x $1\frac{1}{2}$ in.) to make the entrance to the igloo.

IGLOO VILLAGE

This engraving, made in 1871, shows a large Inuit village in the Canadian Arctic. Most Inuit igloos were simple, domelike structures. The Inuit built these temporary shelters during their winter hunting trips.

A COZY HOME

An Inuit hunter shelters inside his igloo. A small entrance tunnel prevents cold winds from entering the shelter and traps warm air inside. Outside, the temperature may be as low as -158°F. Inside, the heat from the stove, candles, and the warmth of the hunter's body keeps the air at around 41°F.

THE FINAL BLOCK

An Inuit hunter carefully places the final block of ice on the roof of his igloo. Ancient hunters used sharp ice knives to shape the blocks so that they fitted together exactly. Any gaps were sealed with snow, to prevent the icy winds from entering the shelter.

Inuit hunters built temporary shelters by fitting ice blocks together to form a spiraling dome structure called an igloo. Only hard-packed snow was used to make the building blocks.

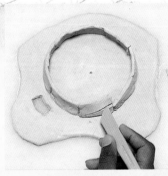

4 Stick nine large blocks around the edge of the circle. Use water to make the clay stick to the base. Cut across two rectangular blocks as shown above.

5 Using your modeling tool, carefully cut a small piece of clay from the corner of each of the remaining blocks, as shown above.

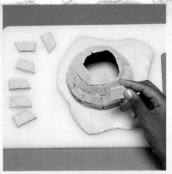

6 Starting from the two blocks cut earlier, build up the walls, slanting each block in as you go. Use the six small blocks at the top. Leave a hole at the top.

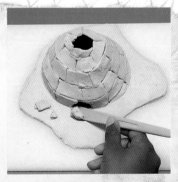

7 Use the modeling tool to form a small entrance to the igloo behind the rectangle already cut into the base. When the clay has dried, paint the igloo white.

Arctic Children

MODEL IGLOO

An Inuit toddler plays with a model igloo at a nursery in the Canadian Arctic. The blocks of wood spiral upward in the same way as the blocks of ice do in a real igloo, so the toy helps modern children to learn the ancient art of building igloos.

CHILDREN WERE AT THE CENTER of most arctic societies. Inuit babies and younger children spent most of their time riding on their mother's back, nestled in a snug pouch called an amaut. The babies of many arctic groups were named for a respected member of the community, and their birth was celebrated with a huge feast. As children grew older, other members of the family helped the mother to bring up her child.

Today, most arctic children go to school when they are young. However, the children of past generations traveled with their parents as the group moved to fresh reindeer pastures or new hunting grounds. Very young boys and girls were treated equally. As they grew up, however, children helped with different tasks and learned the skills that they would need later on in life. Boys learned how to hunt and tend animals. Girls learned to sew and cook, and to work with animal skins.

BIRTHDAY FEAST

Traditional food is prepared at the birthday celebration of the young boy sitting at the table. Parents often named their newborn babies after people who had been respected in the community, such as a great hunter. The baby was thought to inherit that person's skills and personality.

FEEDING BIRDS TOY

You will need: self-drying clay, rolling pin, ruler, modeling tool, board, two toothpicks, white and brown paint, water pot, paint brush.

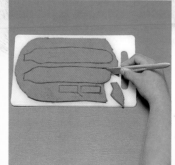

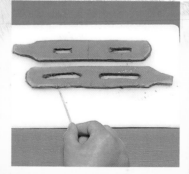

1 Roll out some of the clay into a 8 ³/₄ x 5¹/₂ in. rectangle with a thickness of around ¹/₂ in. Cut out two large paddles (7 x 1¹/₄ in.) and two stalks (1¹/₂ x ³/₄ in.)

2 Cut two slots on paddle 1 (2 x ³/₈ in.) and two on paddle 2 (1 x ³/₈ in.). Use a toothpick to pierce a hole in the side of paddle 1 through these slots.

3 Roll out two egg shapes, each about 2 x 1¹/₄ in., in the palm of your hands. Make two bird heads and stick them to the egg-shaped bodies.

RIDING HIGH

One of the children in this old illustration is being carried in a special hood, called an amaut, high on the back of his mother's jacket. The second child is tucked inside her mother's sealskin boots. However, it was less common for a child to be carried in this way.

LENDING A HAND

A Nenet boy and his younger brother help to feed a reindeer calf that has lost its mother. Fathers taught their sons to handle animals from a very early age. Children were encouraged to care for the family's tame deer and dogs.

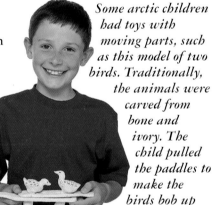

PLAYING WITH DOLLS

A doll dressed in a soft, fleecy coat rests on a Nenet sledge in Arctic Russia. Many arctic girls like to play with dolls, as children do around the world. Traditionally, the dolls' heads were carved from ivory. The doll in the picture, however, is made of modern plastic.

Some arctic children had toys with moving parts, such as this model of two birds. Traditionally, the animals were carved from bone and ivory. The child pulled the paddles to make the birds bob up and down.

4 Stick the stalks you made earlier to the base of each bird's body. Using the toothpick, pierce a small hole through the stalk, close to the body.

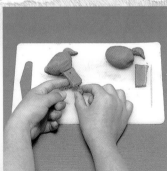

5 Allow the clay bird to dry on its side. You will need to support the stalk with a small piece of clay, to hold the bird upright as it dries.

6 Place the stalk of each bird in the slots in the paddles. Push a toothpick into the holes in the edge of paddle 1, through the stalks and out the other side.

7 Add two small pieces of clay to the bottom of each stalk to keep the birds in place. You can paint the toy once the clay has dried.

ARCTIC CHILDREN   53

Aztec and Mayan Homes

AZTEC AND MAYAN PEOPLE LIVING in Mesoamerica (known today as Central America) used local materials for building. They had no wheeled transportation, so carrying building materials long distances was very difficult. Stone was the most expensive and longest-lasting building material. It was used for religious buildings, rulers' palaces, and tombs. The homes of ordinary people were built more quickly from cheaper materials, such as sun-dried mud bricks, called adobe, or mud smeared over a framework of wooden poles.

All Mesoamerican homes were very simply furnished. There were no chairs or tables, curtains or carpets—just some jars and baskets for storage and a few reed mats. Everyone, from rulers to slaves, sat and slept on mats on the floor. Most ordinary Aztec homes were L-shaped or built around a courtyard, with a separate bathroom for washing and a small shrine to the gods in the main room.

FAMILY HOME

This present-day Mayan family home is built in traditional style, with red-painted, mud and timber walls. It has one door and no windows. The floor is made of pounded earth. The roof, thatched with dried grass, is steeply sloped, so that the rain runs off it.

BURIED UNDERGROUND

Archaeologists have discovered these remains of houses at the Mayan city of Copan. The roofs, walls and doors have rotted away, but we can still see the stone foundations, used to strengthen the walls. The houses are small and tightly packed together.

MAKE A MAYA HOUSE

You will need: thick card, pencil, ruler, scissors, glue, masking tape, terra-cotta plaster paste (or thin plaster, colored with paint), balsa wood strips, water pot, wide gummed paper tape, brush, short pieces of straw.

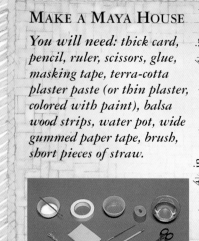

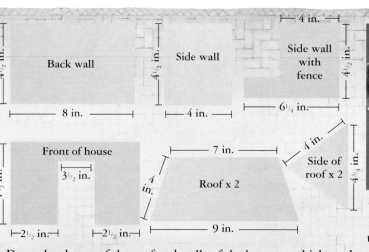

Back wall — 4½ in. × 8 in.
Side wall — 4½ in. × 4 in.
Side wall with fence — 4 in. × 4½ in. × 6¼ in.
Front of house — 4½ in. × 3½ in. — 2½ in. — 2½ in.
Roof x 2 — 7 in. × 4 in. × 9 in.
Side of roof x 2 — 4 in. × 4¾ in.

Draw the shapes of the roof and walls of the house on thick card, using the measurements shown. (Please note that the templates are not shown to scale.) Cut out the pieces.

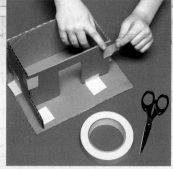

1 Cut out a rectangle 10 x 6 in. from thick card for the base. Stick the house walls and base together with glue. Use masking tape for support.

STONEMASONS AT WORK

Mesoamerican masons constructed massive buildings using very simple equipment. Their wedges were made from wood, and their mallets and hammers were shaped from hard volcanic stone. Until around A.D. 900, metal tools were unknown. Fine details were added by polishing stonework with wet sand.

PLASTER

Big stone buildings, such as temples, were often covered with a kind of plaster called stucco. This was then painted with ornate designs. Plaster was made by burning limestone and mixing it with water and colored earth. By the 1400s, there was so much new building in Tenochtitlan, that the surrounding lake became polluted with chemicals from the plastermaking.

plaster

limestone

SKILLFUL STONEWORK

This carved stone panel from the Mayan city of Chichen-Itza is decorated with a pattern of crosses. It was used to provide a fine facing to thick walls made of rubble and rough stone. This wall decorates a palace building.

A Mayan house provided a cool shelter from the very hot Mexican sun, in addition to keeping out the rain.

2 Paint the walls and base with plaster paste. This will make them look like sun-dried mud. You could also decorate the doorway with balsa wood strips.

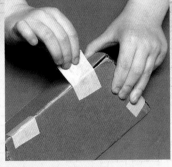

3 Put the house on one side to dry. Take your roof pieces and stick them together with glue. Use masking tape to support the roof, as shown.

4 Moisten the wide paper tape and use it to cover the joints between the roof pieces. There should be no gaps. Then cover the whole roof with glue.

5 Press pieces of straw into the glue on the roof. Work in layers, starting at the bottom. Overlap the layers. Attach the roof to the house using glue.

Mesoamerican Families

FAMILIES WERE very important to the Maya and Aztecs. By working together, family members provided themselves with food, jobs, companionship, and a home. Each member of a family had special responsibilities. Men produced food or earned the money to buy it. Women cared for babies and the home. From the age of about five or six, children were expected to do their share of the family's work by helping their parents. Because family life was so important, marriages were often arranged by a young couple's parents, or by a matchmaker. The role of matchmaker would be played by an old woman who knew both families well. Boys and girls got married when they were between 16 and 20 years old. The young couple usually lived in the boy's parents' home.

Aztec families belonged to local clan groups, known as calpulli. Each calpulli chose its own leader, collected its own taxes, and built its own temple. It offered help to needy families, but also kept a close eye on how members behaved. If someone broke the law, the whole clan might be punished for that person's actions.

MOTHER AND SON
These Mayan clay figures may show a mother and her son. Boys from noble families went to school at about 15. They learned reading, writing, math, astronomy, and religion.

PAINFUL PUNISHMENT
This codex painting shows a father holding his son over a fire of burning chilies as a punishment. Aztec parents used severe punishments in an attempt to make their children honest and obedient members of society.

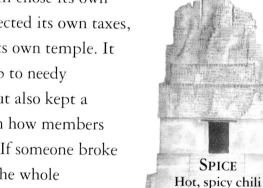

SPICE
Hot, spicy chili peppers were an essential part of many Mayan and Aztec meals. In fact, the Aztecs said that if a meal lacked chilies, it was a fast, not a feast! Chilies were used in stews and in spicy sauces, and they were used in medicine, too. They were crushed and rubbed on aching muscles, or mixed with salt to ease toothaches.

red chilies

dried chilies, preserved for winter use

green chilies

IXTILTON
This Aztec mask is made from a black volcanic stone called obsidian. It shows the god Ixtilton, the helper of Huitzilopochtli, the Aztecs' special tribal god. Aztec legends told how Ixtilton could bring darkness and peaceful sleep to tired children.

HUSBAND AND WIFE
The bride and groom in this codex picture of an Aztec wedding have their clothes tied together. This shows that their lives are now joined. Aztec weddings were celebrated with presents and feasting. Guests carried bunches of flowers, and the bride wore special make-up, with her cheeks painted yellow or red. During the ceremony, the bride and groom sat side by side on a mat in front of the fire.

GUARDIAN GODDESS
The goddess Tlazolteotl is shown in this codex picture. She was the goddess of lust and sin. Tlazolteotl was also said to watch over mothers and young children. Childbirth was the most dangerous time in a woman's life, and women who died in childbirth were honored like brave soldiers.

LEARNING FOR LIFE
A mother teaches her young daughter to cook in this picture from an Aztec codex. The girl is making tortillas, which are flat corn (maize) pancakes. You can see her grinding the corn in a metate (grinding stone) using a mano (stone used with the metate). Aztec mothers and fathers trained their children in all the skills they would need to survive in adult life. Children from the families of expert craftspeople usually learned their parents' special skills.

An Incan House

THE INCAS BEGAN AS A SMALL TRIBE living in the Andes mountains of Peru in South America. Like the Aztec and Maya, the Incas preferred to build their homes from stone. White granite was the best, since it is very hard. The roof of each house was pitched at a very steep angle, so that heavy mountain rains could drain off quickly. Timber roof beams were lashed to stone pegs on the gables, and supported by a wooden frame. This was thatched with a tough grass called ichu.

Most houses had just one story, but a few had two or three, joined by rope ladders inside the house, or by stone blocks set into the outside wall. Most had a single doorway that was hung with cloth or hide.

Each building was home to a single family and formed part of a compound. As many as half a dozen houses would be grouped around a shared courtyard. All the buildings belonged to families who were members of the same ayllu, or clan.

MUD AND THATCH
Various types of houses were to be seen in different parts of the Inca Empire. Many were built in old-fashioned and regional styles. These round and rectangular houses in Bolivia are made of mud bricks (adobe). The houses are thatched with ichu grass.

upper story

inside hearth

courtyard

FLOATING HOMES
These houses are built by the Uru people, who fish in Lake Titicaca, in the southern part of Peru, and hunt in the surrounding marshes. They live on the lake shore and also on floating islands made of matted totora reeds. Their houses are made of totora and ichu grass. Both these materials would have been used in the Titicaca area in Incan times. The reeds are collected from the shallows and piled on the floor of the lake. New reeds are constantly added.

PICTURES AND POTTERY

Houses with pitched roofs and windows appear as part of the decoration on this pottery from Pacheco, Nazca, in Peru. To find out about houses in ancient Peru, historians look at surviving towns and ruins, at housing styles still in use today and at old pictures and designs on objects.

Squared-off blocks of stone are called ashlars. These white granite ashlars make up a wall in the Incan town of Pisaq. They are topped by a round stone peg. Pegs like these were probably used to support roof beams or other structures, such as ladders from one story to another.

gable

roof beam

roof peg

wall niche

BUILDING MATERIALS

The materials used to build an Incan house depended on local supplies. Rock was the favorite material. White granite, dark basalt, and limestone were used whenever it was possible. Away from the mountains, clay was made into bricks and dried hard in the sun to make adobe. Roof beams were formed from timber poles. Thatch was made of grass or reed.

clay   *white granite*

thatch   *timber*

BUILDING TO LAST

The Incas built simple, but solid, dwellings in the mountains. The massive boulders used for temples and fortresses are here replaced by smaller, neatly cut stones. Notice how the roof beams are lashed to the gables to support the thatch. Stone roofs were very rare, even on the grandest houses. Timber joists provide an upper story. The courtyard is used just as much as the inside of the house for everyday living.

Married Life in Incan Times

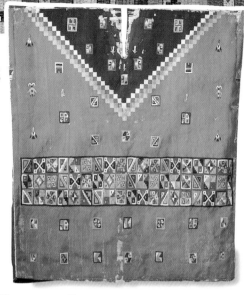

WEDDINGS WERE SOME of the happiest occasions in an Incan village. They offered a chance for the whole community to take time off of work. The day was celebrated with dancing, music, and feasting. The groom would probably be 25 years of age, at which point he was regarded as an adult citizen, and his bride would be a little younger—about 20.

For the first year of the marriage, a couple did not have to pay any taxes, either in goods or labor. However, most of their lives would be spent working hard. When they were elderly, they would still be expected to help with household chores. Even later, when they became too old or sick to take care of themselves, they received free food and clothes from the State warehouse. They would then be cared for by their clan or family group.

Not everyone was expected to get married. The mamakuna (virgins of the sun) lived much like nuns, in a special convent in the Incan town of Cuzco. They wove fine cloth and carried out religious duties. No men were allowed to enter the mamakuna's building.

WEDDING CLOTHES
An Inca nobleman would get married in a very fine tunic. This one is from the southern coast of Peru. Commoners had to wear simpler clothes, but couples were presented with free new clothes from the State warehouses when they married.

MARRIAGE PROSPECTS
Two Inca noblewomen are painted on the side of this kero (wooden beaker). Women of all social classes were only allowed to marry with the approval of their parents and of State officials. They were expected to remain married for life, and divorce was forbidden. If either the husband or wife was unfaithful, he or she could face trial and might even be put to death.

REAL PEOPLE
This jar is over 1,300 years old. Unlike the portraits on many jars, it seems to show a real person sitting down and thinking about life. It reminds us that ancient cultures and civilizations were made up of individuals who fell in love, raised children, and grew old, just as people do today.

A ROYAL MARRIAGE

A prince of the emperor's family marries in Cuzco. The scene is imagined by an artist of the 1800s. An emperor had many secondary wives in addition to his sister-empress. Between them, they produced many princes and princesses. Incan royal families were divided by jealousy and by complicated relations, which often resulted in open warfare. The emperor ordered his officials to keep tight control over who married whom. His own security on the throne depended on it.

A HOME OF THEIR OWN

When a couple married, they left their parents' houses and moved into their own home, like this one at Machu Picchu, in the Andes. The couple now took official control of the fields they would work. These had been allocated to the husband when he was born. Most couples stayed in the area occupied by their own clan, so their relatives would remain nearby.

HIS AND HERS

The everyday lives of most married couples in the Inca Empire were taken up by hard work. Men and women were expected to do different jobs. Women made the chicha beer and did the cooking, weaving, and some field work. Men did field work and fulfiled the mit'a labor tax in service to the Inca State. They might build irrigation channels or repair roads.

Glossary

A

adobe Plaster made from clay and straw, used by Pueblo people of Central America, Egyptians, and Mesopotamians on their homes.

agriculture Farming—the activity of growing crops and breeding animals.

amaut Black pouch used by Inuit people of the north American Arctic to carry babies and young children.

ancestor An individual from whom one is descended, such as a great-great-grandfather.

archaeologist A person who studies ancient remains or ruins.

atrium The hallway or courtyard of a Roman house. The middle of the atrium was open to the sky.

Aztecs Mesoamerican people who lived in northern and central Mexico. They were at their most powerful btween A.D. 1350 and A.D. 1520.

B

banquet A rich, elaborate feast served with great ceremony.

brahmins The priests, members of the first caste in India.

bronze A metal made from a mixture of copper and tin.

C

calpulli An Aztec family or neighborhood group. The calpulli enforced law and order. It arranged education, training, and welfare benefits for its members.

caste One of four social classes into which Hindus in India were divided.

civil servant An official who carries out government administration.

codex An Aztec folding book.

Confucianism The Western name for the teachings of the Chinese philosopher Kong Fuzi (Confucius), which call for social respect for one's family and ancestors.

cremation The burning of dead bodies.

D

dowry Money that is given to a newly married couple, usually by the bride's father.

dynasty A period of rule by the same royal family, such as the pharaohs of Egypt and the rulers in the Chinese empire.

F

faience A type of opaque glass that is often blue or green. It is made from quartz or sand, lime, ash, and natron.

feud
feud A long-standing quarrel, especially between two families.

H

hunter-gatherer A person who lives by hunting animals and gathering wild roots and plants for food.

I

igloo An Inuit word meaning "house," which is often used to refer to Inuit shelters built from ice or snow blocks.

imperial Relating to the rule of an emperor or empress.

Inuit The native people of the North American Arctic, Canada, and Greenland, as distinguished from those of Asia and the Aleutian Islands. Inuit is also the general name for an Eskimo in Canada.

K

kero An Incan drinking vessel.

kimono A loose robe with wide sleeves, worn by both men and women in Japan.

L

longhouse The chief building of a Viking homestead.

loom A wooden frame used for weaving cloth.

lyre A harplike instrument.

M

maki sushi Rolls of vinegared rice made with fish and vegetable fillings.

Maya People who lived in southeastern Mexico, Guatamala, and Belize.

millet A grass-type plant that produces edible seeds.

mosaic A picture made up of many small squares or cubes of glass, stone, or pottery, and set in soft concrete.

mummy A human, or sometimes animal, body preserved by drying.

N

Nenet A reindeer herding people of southern Siberia.

New Kingdom The period of Egyptian history between 1550–1070 B.C.

O

oppida The Roman name for fortified Celtic towns.

P

papyrus A tall reed that grows in the river Nile, used to make a kind of paper by the ancient Egyptians.

paratha A fried wheat bread eaten in northern India.

pharaoh A ruler of ancient Egypt.

prehistoric Belonging to the time before written records were made.

Pueblo People from the southwest of Mexico who lived in villages built of mud and stone.

pyramid A large pointed monument with a broad, square base and four triangular sides.

Q

quern A simple machine, made from two stones, that is used to grind corn.

R

relief A carved stone slab.

S

scribe A professional writer, a clerk, or civil servant.

T

tablet A flat piece of clay of various shapes and sizes, used for writing.

tablinium The formal reception room and study in a Roman house.

taboo A rule or custom linked with shamanic tribal religious beliefs that shows respect to the spirits.

temple A special building used for worshipping a god.

terra-cotta Brown-red earthen ware used for making pots and sculpture.**textile** Any cloth that has been woven, such as silk or cotton.

textile Any cloth that has been woven, such as silk or cotton.

threshing To beat or thrash out grain from corn.

tipi Conical tent with a frame of poles, covered with animal skins, used by the Native North American Plains people.

tribe A group of people who share a common language and way of life.

triclinium The dining room in a Roman house.

V

Viking A member of the Scandinavian peoples who lived by sea-raiding in the early Middle Ages.

W

warrior A man who fights in wars.

wigwam A Native American house made of bark, rushes, or skins, spread over arched poles that were lashed together.

winnowing Separating grains of wheat and rice from their papery outer layer, called chaff.

Index

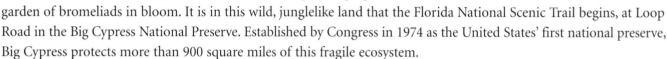

Big Cypress

"It's getting deep!"

Behind me, several hikers enjoy their first immersion into the Big Cypress ecosystem. When we started out along Sawmill Road, I was surprised to see the exposed slabs of limestone that make up the footpath. I'd expected a wet hike. But the Florida Trail never disappoints. In less than half a mile, we encounter puddles enveloping the old cypress-plank road. I chuckle as I watch hikers try to skirt the puddles, and I plunge in. A few minutes later, the folks behind me join suit, laughing as they slosh through shin-deep water.

I t is a haunting place. Wizened dwarf cypresses rise from broad sawgrass prairies. Deep solution holes puncture flat slabs of bone-white limestone karst. Black water flows beneath dense stands of lichen-covered cypresses, each tree hosting a hanging garden of bromeliads in bloom. It is in this wild, junglelike land that the Florida National Scenic Trail begins, at Loop Road in the Big Cypress National Preserve. Established by Congress in 1974 as the United States' first national preserve, Big Cypress protects more than 900 square miles of this fragile ecosystem.

Described by Florida Trail founder Jim Kern as a landscape comparable in its stark beauty to the Serengeti in Africa, the Big Cypress encompasses more than a million acres of cypress strands, deep sloughs, and open prairies. Gentle erosion of the spongy limestone bedrock created the strands and sloughs through which the seasonal rains flow toward the sea. Each narrow slough acts as a creek, channeling the rains, while the broad, vast strands host thickets of cypress. The perpetual humidity and warmth encourage epiphytes to blanket the trees. Big Cypress hosts more rare species of bromeliads and orchids than any other place in Florida.

The trail forms a narrow corridor through a vast landscape. Around us are eerie pond cypresses, dwarfed by their inability to gather nutrients from the marl. Yellow and purple bladderworts thrive in the prairies, their blooms adding splashes of color to the gray-green landscape. It's spring, and the cypresses look puffy with their new green needles. The cardinal wild pine is in bloom, its spiky red blossoms beckoning us to gaze up at the aerial gardens in each cypress strand. We can tell the water is low right now. The periphyton, a living mat of algae, bacteria, and fungi, lies stretched in a thin web across the cypresses' knees. When hydrated, it becomes a thick goop, providing a food source for microscopic invertebrates.

As we emerge onto one of the marl prairies, I notice our leader, Chuck Wilson, start to slip and slide. He grins. "It feels like walking on Crisco." I'm glad I have a hiking stick to steady myself, or I'd have fallen already. The slick marl is tricky to walk on, and when the periphyton gets a little wet, it adds more greasiness to the mix.

"I'm down!" A hiker hits the muck, and I'm reminded of the chaos along the edge of an ice-skating rink. I turn around to assist but he's sitting there, laughing, as his wife catches up. "The trick is to pull your shoe out and still have your foot in it," she says. Our chain of 15 hikers stretches across the prairie like a giant caterpillar, sloshing and slopping and crunching our way along this very different sort of footpath. For thru-hikers, it's a challenging start to a 1,300-mile backpacking trip through the state of Florida, and it might explain why the Florida Trail doesn't see too many of them.

Most hikers dip into sections of the trail on their wilderness outings, enjoying long weekends and day hikes as they traverse more than 80 distinct habitats between Big Cypress and Pensacola, the blessing of Florida's vast biodiversity. Lots of them are folks like these, out on an organized excursion with an experienced leader, looking for a taste

Above: Quill-leaf bromeliad
Opposite: Florida Trail heading north through a cypress swamp

of adventure on a day trip. During the rainy season from summer through fall, the Big Cypress Swamp averages 60 inches of rain, which is why most hikers tackle this section of trail in the dry season each spring. But "dry" is relative. "Is there anyone left with dry boots?" Chuck asks as we gather together near the 3-mile marker. The smiling crowd shakes their heads—"No."

For several miles, Chuck tells us there will be a dry spot "just a little ways up the trail." I begin to doubt his words, but then we rise into a hammock of wax myrtle and cabbage palm, bay and sawgrass. It's the Frog Hammock campsite, with logs and concrete blocks for weary hikers to perch on while eating lunch. One fellow takes off his waterproof boots and pours out the water that slipped in from the top. "There's not much use to that," I say. I try dumping sand from my shoes, but I know it's just as futile. Not far beyond Frog Hammock, the water becomes knee-deep, and rain starts to patter down. I hear shouts of glee from the hikers behind me as they slip and splash into deeper water beneath the colorful bromeliads.

The sky fills with dark clouds, and a sudden icy blast reminds us that a storm front is about to blow through here, changing the character of our hike. Behind me, Ann comes to a sudden stop. "I almost lost my shoe on that one!" As she pulls it out of the muck, she discovers the sole of her running shoe is peeling off. I whip out the duct tape and her husband manages an emergency repair, wrapping her shoe in a silvery cocoon. We see signs of wildlife: scratches on cypress trunks from bobcats and, pressed deep into the marl, the prints of raccoons and deer.

Then all is still, save the sloshing of hikers. I pull one mucky shoe out of the water and turn to Jan. "Funny thing, when I was five years old, my mother would punish me for coming home with mud on my clothes. I'd have to sit at the table and write 'I will not stomp in mud puddles' a hundred times." Jan grins. "Of course," I continue, sloshing into the next puddle, "it's fun now to remind her what I do for a living."

At Robert's Strand, the texture of the landscape changes. Following a natural garden path of giant limestone pavers, we enter a lush thicket of tropical trees with giant sword ferns towering overhead. It's easy to lose sight of one

another. "This way!" someone shouts, the depths of the fern jungle swallowing her up. I poke my hiking stick into a deep solution hole as I work my way through the ever-darkening forest, emerging at the edge of a blackwater slough. Time to wade! It's an obstacle course of water and fallen trees as we cross the strand on slender islands, ducking around pond apple trees and the stumps of giant cypresses. We pass a rounded mound of earth and humus rising high above the dark waters, the type of place a bull gator would choose for a lookout. "It's wet up here!" Virginia shouts as we leave the strand for the next stretch of cypress forest. As the low spot in the forest, the trail is inundated with water.

Jan freezes. "Snake!" Several hikers have already passed this spot. John walks up to survey the scene, and I'm not far behind. "Stay back!" he warns, poking around with his hiking stick. I caution him to be careful. A closer look poses a real dilemma: There is not one snake, but two, and they're both cottonmouth moccasins, aggressive and dangerous. Like Scylla and Charybdis, they flank the footpath, one a

Exposed limestone karst makes up the footpath

dusky charcoal, the other a deep, rich brown. Both snakes lie coiled and silent, facing away from the footpath. Gathering up some nerve, I walk straight between them, and the other hikers follow suit. Neither snake stirs. Within a few minutes, Jan stops again. "Snake!" Curled up in the footpath, the light-patterned cottonmouth is nearly imperceptible against the mud—until it opens its mouth to reveal its white interior. Several people stepped right over it without even seeing it. We give it a wide berth.

In hues of peppermint and butterscotch, lozenge-shaped ramshorn snail shells bob in the murky mud puddles. A whisk fern grows out of a hollow in a cypress trunk. Spiky crimson blooms emerge from the octopus-like forms of the potbellied air plants clinging to young cypresses. The bottom of Ann's shoe comes off again, and she has to wrap it twice with duct tape to keep going. Obstacles hidden by the knee-deep water trip us up: slippery logs and the remains of old cypress stumps, the ancient forebears of the cypresses that surround us today.

"Log!" I shout, stepping over yet another submerged log and into a hole more than knee-deep. "Deeper water!" Calls ring out through the forest as folks give similar warnings to their fellow hikers behind them. We pass Mile Marker 7 and emerge onto a marl prairie under dwarf cypresses. I breathe a sigh of relief. "I can see my car!"

Six hours after we started at Loop Road, we emerge at the Oasis Ranger Station, mud-splattered and weary but happy. From here, experienced hikers can take on a three- or four-

Above: Alligator sunning itself
Right: Dwarf pond cypresses rise
from a sawgrass prairie

day backpacking trip north along the Florida Trail through more of the Big Cypress National Preserve to Alligator Alley, traversing nearly 30 miles of some of Florida's most remote landscapes.

As I wait in line at the water spigot to wash the mud off my shoes, I watch the parade of cars whizzing down US 41 through the heart of the Big Cypress Swamp. A scenic panorama of sawgrass and dwarf cypress stretches out to the horizon. Viewed at 60 miles per hour, those expanses diminish in size and grandeur. The flocks of rare white pelicans become mere dots in the salt flats, and the endangered Florida panthers that lope across the highway risk their lives to wander their territory. To experience the Big Cypress, to immerse yourself in the environment, to feel it in your shoes and on your clothes, you truly have to hike the trail.

Above: Male painted bunting
Below: Southern terminus of the Florida Trail along Loop Road
Opposite: A cabbage palm flatwoods near 10 Mile Camp

Seminole Country

Phyllis Malinski and I looked sadly out the window as I drove down Government Road through Big Cypress Seminole Reservation. Sporting an unusually light spotted coat, a bobcat lay sprawled across the road, a victim of an automobile in the night. Or was it a young panther? We'd never know. It was a morning for wildlife watching, but not in a way we'd planned. Approaching the village, I slowed down for something sitting in the road—a 5-foot alligator. Behind me, Paul slowed down, too. But the gator figured he'd had enough traffic and scuttled under Paul's pickup. I watched in the rearview mirror. Thankfully, the gator made it safely to the other side of the road.

Ah, the joys of section hiking: a drive of nearly 45 miles each way to place one vehicle at both ends of a 12-mile segment of the Florida Trail. With all three of us in my car, I headed back along Government Road to I-75, this time stopping for what looked like a deer carcass surrounded by vultures. It turned out to be a massive alligator fighting the vultures for possession of a dead armadillo. Upon hearing my car, the gator turned tail and ran, diving for the canal with a mighty splash.

Many of the original inhabitants of Florida—including the Ais, Apalachee, Calusa, Jeaga, and Timucua—died off after their interactions with Spanish explorers in the 1500s, victims of common European diseases for which the tribal members had no immunity. Spreading southward through the Southeast, Creek and Maskókî tribes intermixed with the survivors. Joined by free blacks and runaway slaves, they began a distinct culture and came to be known as the Seminoles. In his *Travels,* William Bartram included the first documented visits to the Seminole villages of Cuscowilla, along modern-day Paynes Prairie, and Talahasochte, along the Suwannee River, in 1774.

As early as 1812, conflicts broke out across the Florida Territory as white settlers pushed south into Seminole lands. When Florida became a U.S. territory in 1821, more than 5,000 Native Americans lived across the peninsula. To facilitate settlement of Florida, the federal government forced the Seminoles to sign a treaty to give up their claims to Florida in exchange for a reservation that blanketed the southern part of the peninsula, the "useless" lands south of the southernmost Seminole settlement. Although they had no desire to live in the swamps, the Seminoles acquiesced.

As anti-American sentiment grew within the tribes, some of them decided to strike back. Sparked by the simultaneous ambush of Indian Agent Wiley Thompson at Fort King in Ocala and of a force of U.S. soldiers walking the Fort King Road near the Wahoo Swamp, the Second Seminole War lasted longer than any other war fought by U.S. citizens: seven years, ending in 1842 without a peace treaty. It was a bitter struggle between the U.S. Army, attempting to remove the Seminoles to "Indian Lands" in Oklahoma by coercion, trickery, or force, and the Seminoles who wanted to stay in Florida or die here. Following the lead of medicine man Abiaka (known as Sam Jones to the U.S. Army), the surviving Seminoles melted into the tree islands of the Everglades and the hammocks of Big Cypress, where the Army dared not follow.

Heading north along the Florida Trail through Big Cypress National Preserve, hikers pass through the lands the Seminoles have occupied for more than a century. Roads used for logging and oil exploration crisscross the northern extent of the preserve, and it is on these roads that the Florida Trail works its way from Alligator Alley to the Big Cypress Seminole Reservation.

Stunted pond cypresses grow amid expanses of sawgrass, while tall cypresses line a manmade canal created to drain swampland and provide fill for Nobles Road. It's spring, and everything is in bloom. Florida petunias lift their purple blossoms to the sun, and black-eyed Susans wave in the breeze. A red-tailed hawk cries out from its perch in a tall cypress, its form half-hidden by a profusion of flowery crimson spikes on the cardinal wild pine. In what seems

Above: Eastern pondhawk dragonfly
Opposite: A palm hammock along the trail

like very little time, we're in the thick of the wild. Although we're tempted eastward by a side trail—a backpacking loop created for a wilder look at this environment—we must stick to the main trail today.

Clouds darken overhead as we reach a confusing intersection. I lead us to the left as the rain starts pouring down. "It's a dead end. Damn." As we struggle back to the main trail, a deer regards us through the raindrops. Walking under a canopy of tropical trees, we follow a befuddled wild turkey down the footpath. Either it can't fly in the rain, or it's not very bright. Every few minutes, it turns around and looks at us, then continues running ahead. The rain slacks off, and we start to think about food. "All hikes are better when there's food at the end," says Phyllis, echoing the general sentiment in the Florida Trail Association. I'd love to have a dollar for every time I've heard someone say, "We're an eating club with a hiking disorder."

The cabbage palm flatwoods around us remind me of the adjoining Florida Panther National Wildlife Refuge, recalling the fact that we're in prime panther territory. In 1896, naturalist Charles B. Cory wrote *Hunting and Fishing in Florida,* and in it, he classified this now highly endangered mammal as a subspecies of cougar. In his honor, this tawny-coated species bears the name *Puma concolor coryi.* The highest concentration of Florida panthers exists in the Big Cypress and Everglades; scattered individuals have been spotted in other parts of the state. While females roam a territory of 80 square miles, males are known to wander up to 200 square miles. The population of Florida panthers barely tops 70 members, so Texas cougars have been imported to help mix up the dangerously inbred gene pool. Although the panthers are large carnivores, they're shy about approaching humans. It's been hikers, of course, who've reported panther sightings along the Florida Trail, especially in the Big Cypress. We're not so lucky today.

At the gate into the Big Cypress Seminole Reservation, we pause for photos. Not long after the Second Seminole War, a third war came on the heels of a Seminole attack on a trading post on the Peace River, at the northern boundary of their lands. This time, the U.S. Army entered the swamps, burned villages, and destroyed the beloved banana plantation of Chief Billy Bowlegs. The Seminoles who did not surrender vanished even deeper into the Everglades. By 1858, less than 300 Seminoles remained in Florida, withdrawn from all contact with white settlers. They are the ancestors of the Seminole and Miccosukee of today.

In the 1950s, when Congress began cutting federal aid to Native Americans, the majority of Florida's Seminoles adopted a constitutional form of government and organized as a corporation, the Seminole Tribe of Florida. In 1962, speakers of the Mikisúkî language who lived along the Tamiami Trail (US 41) banded together to form the Miccosukee Tribe of Indians of Florida.

Encompassing 50,000 acres, the Big Cypress Seminole Reservation is the largest of seven reservations scattered

Above: Red-shouldered hawk
Left: Hut with traditional Seminole grass thatch roof
Opposite: Thicket swamp at Billie Swamp Safari

across South Florida. Thanks to the tribe's good graces, the Florida Trail passes through the Seminole Tribe of Florida's private lands. Hikers traversing this section must preregister with the Seminole Tribe through the Florida Trail Association before undertaking a hike.

It was inside the reservation that my friend Deb Blick spotted her first panther, just two days after my hike. "I was sitting in the cab getting my GPS ready," says Deb, "when I glanced at the rearview mirror and said, 'Dang, I think that's a panther!'" Deb stepped out onto the running board to snap some photos. After the panther checked one route, she came back out to the road and "continued straight toward me for another hundred feet…looking right at me like she was curious as to what appendage was stuck to the side of the truck."

As for *our* dangerous creatures, Phyllis discovers herself under attack. Positioned defensively in the middle of the trail, a little crawdad swipes its claws at her hiking boots, giving us all a chuckle. Our weary bodies are buoyed by banter of what might be on the menu at the Swamp Water Café. Crawdad, perhaps?

After reaching Paul's truck, we head up the road for a meal. The parking lot is packed at Billie Swamp Safari, where visitors wander through a zoo of native creatures and board airboats and swamp buggies for excursions into the swamps. Most of the reservation's roadside lands have been converted to residential or agricultural areas, but out here, the haunting cypress forests and sawgrass remain. A pack of Boy Scouts spills out of traditional Seminole chickees along the edge of the marsh. A visit to Billie Swamp Safari and the Ah-Tah-Thi-Ki Museum, both along the route of the Florida Trail, provides insight into Seminole culture and history in the context of the Big Cypress.

The food comes in copious quantities at the Swamp Water Café, the Indian taco on traditional flatbread massive enough to satisfy our hungry hiker appetites. It takes that sort of fuel to get across the reservation, another 15 miles of following the orange blazes along the reservation roads to connect to the next section of the Florida Trail, which heads north along the L-3 Canal.

The Forgotten Everglades

"Look! There's a spoonbill!"

Bob and Paul stopped short as we caught sight of two roseate spoonbills working their way along the L-3 Canal, the birds' pink plumage a stark contrast against the dark water. Surrounding us was a remnant of the original Everglades, preserved within the Rotenberger Wildlife Management Area. Backpacking on a January weekend, we'd just started a 37-mile Florida Trail section from the northern boundary of the Big Cypress Seminole Reservation to Lake Okeechobee. And here, we made our first true acquaintance with the forgotten Everglades. Willow marshes stretched off to the horizon. Reddish egrets picked their way through spiky grasses. Yellow-crowned night herons stood watch over rookery nests. Although drab in its winter colors, the marsh teemed with wildlife.

◆ ◆ ◆ ◆ ◆ ◆ ◆

Except for thru-hikers and the dedicated trail crew from the Happy Hoofers Chapter of the Florida Trail Association, few ever walk this remote section of trail. Although it's only a small portion of the hike, the Rotenberger Wildlife Management Area turned out to be an enormous surprise. I didn't think there were any natural places left in this part of Florida. But it was over far too soon. The wonder of the real Everglades, the land the Seminoles knew by heart, yielded to a landscape best indexed as "Everglades, former." The drained lands. Sliced and diced by a grid of canals large and small into cattle ranches and sugarcane fields within the last century. Having reread Patrick Smith's Florida epic *A Land Remembered* just a week before, I could imagine the vast marsh reaching south from Lake Okeechobee, crowded with custard apple trees. Perched on a limestone shelf that slopes toward Florida Bay, these lands provided a natural drainage for Lake Okeechobee to pour its overflow into the sea.

Along came Hamilton Disston. In 1881, he headed a grand scheme to drag Florida out of its post–Civil War insolvency: He would drain 12 million acres of "submerged lands" in South Florida in exchange for 6 million acres. He also purchased 4 million acres of land scattered from Titusville to Marco Island in the largest-ever land purchase made by any individual in the world at that time. It cost a million dollars—not chicken feed in those days, but well below the value of the land. Egged on by Governor Napoleon Bonaparte Broward, whose "Save the Everglades" campaign meant "for agricultural use," Disston established the Okeechobee Land Company to drain the Everglades and "straighten out" the rivers flowing in and out of Lake Okeechobee for commerce.

With its tropical rivers turned into navigable ditches, the settlement of South Florida's interior commenced. The deep muck hidden beneath the Everglades proved ideal for farming. Sugarcane became the largest cash crop of the region.

We walk for a day along the L-3 and L-2 Canals, which were once natural sloughs draining Lake Okeechobee into the Big Cypress Swamp. They are long gashes in the landscape, separating cattle ranches to the west from cane fields to the east. But some of the wildlife remains. Turtles poke their noses out of the dark water. A flock of glossy ibises wings overhead. Leaping across an open field, a bobcat vanishes behind the stalks of sugarcane. Using the dike as a windbreak, we pitch our tents along the L-2 Canal, watching sunset sparkle across the water. Night falls fast and cold. In the morning, frost coats everything.

◆ ◆ ◆ ◆ ◆ ◆ ◆

"Why don't we head up to the wayside park?" Paul points it out on the map. "It would be a great place to cook breakfast." Bob and I agree. It's 7 miles away, but it's 7 flat miles along the dike. The sun pours through the flowering

Above: A raccoon in the Rotenberger WMA
Opposite: Sugarcane and wildflowers along the L-2 Canal Road

tips of the tall cane, setting them aflame before it rises into the clear blue sky. At the wayside, we spread out our tents to dry and attempt to make breakfast as the cane trucks rumble past at high speed, spraying clouds of cinders. It's Sunday, but cane harvesting goes on seven days a week during the season, October through March. Nearly 25 percent of the sugar consumed in the United States comes from these fields, the crops spreading out over 450,000 acres south and east of Lake Okeechobee.

Rotated with some of the sugarcane plantings are rice fields, flooded during the growing season with just enough water to stimulate the rice and attract waterfowl. As we hike above the edge of a flooded field, we spot two crested caracaras involved in an elaborate display of hopping and flapping, either a fight or a mating ritual. Although members of the falcon family, these unusual raptors are almost parrotlike, with red faces and thick, curved bills. They are Mexico's national birds.

Bird life abounds in the sugar fields, and we hear deer crashing through the tall cane as we pick out our next evening's encampment. Behind us is a recently burned field, where the rumble of harvesters and trucks goes on well into

the night. The slightly warmer weather could coax alligators from their muddy burrows, so Bob warns me about filtering water at dusk: "When you're leaning over the canal at dusk, the alligators figure you look like a deer." I hurry at my task.

As we make the final turn toward Lake Harbor, the trail parallels the Miami Canal. Like a scene from an Alfred Hitchcock movie, thousands of blackbirds wheel through the freshly burned cane. Harvesters stand at the ready, resembling a gathering of brontosaurs.

Human intervention has permanently altered this landscape. Only a few hammocks of royal palms surrounding some of the home-steads hint at the natural glory of the original Everglades. Walking along the dark canal, I think about the rivers that once were, the tropics that naturalist Charles Torrey Simpson explored in the early 1900s. My heart aches for South Florida, its paradise lost.

Above: Aerial view of sugarcane fields
Right: Tricolored heron
Opposite, top: Harvesting sugarcane along the Florida Trail
Opposite: Sunrise over newly planted sugarcane

The Big O

A solemn crowd stands on the Herbert Hoover Dike at South Bay, watching three young girls. Hair blowing in the wind, they sow handfuls of their grandmother's ashes across the Florida Trail.

For three years, Sunny Piskura pestered me at every Florida Trail Association conference. "You have to come hike the Big O, Sandy!" I'd nod and say, "As soon as I have the time." When I finally made plans in 2002 to join the annual event that the Loxahatchee Chapter had been putting on for the last decade, Sunny was elated.

And then she died, less than three months before the Big O event, a vibrant volunteer felled by a swift-moving cancer. For nine years, she'd led the hike.

Under sunny skies, the brisk breeze off Lake Okeechobee scattered her ashes across the dike.

◆ ◆ ◆ ◆ ◆ ◆ ◆

The challenge: walking 109 miles in nine days, a full circle on the Florida Trail around Lake Okeechobee, the second-largest lake entirely within the United States. The walk is on a rugged limestone dike with no shade. The reality: It's a blast. With logistics worked out in advance by a dedicated crew of volunteers, all I had to do was hike. Each evening, we'd camp at a campground and have a group dinner at a local restaurant. No backpack, no meal prep, no fuss. Just put one foot in front of the other and make it to the shuttle at the end of each day's hike.

Day 1 always starts out with a hefty crowd thanks to the Wimp Walk, instituted to enable hikers with less stamina to be a part of the opening-day experience. Swaddled in multiple layers of warm clothing, part of that crowd surrounds me as we approach the swinging drawbridge at Belle Glade. I marvel at the energy of the children who race up and down the dike to play hide-and-seek in the cane fields. Hidden in these particular fields lie the Chosen Mounds, a multilayered burial complex unearthed by Smithsonian researchers in the 1930s. In addition to the bones of the ancient Calusa, a seagoing people, diggers found porpoise teeth used for engraving, conchs used as hoes, and thousands of potsherds.

But where's the lake? All I see is a broad canal lined with dead melaleuca and Australian pine. The U.S. Army Corps of Engineers killed these invasive species two years ago, creating vast ghost forests. In my hand I heft my hiking stick, a sturdy piece of Australian pine fashioned by my friend Warren into a useful tool. I know I've seen melaleuca mulch, so why leave these trees standing? I soon have my answer. Several hikers—including Gordon Johnson, the founder of the Big O hike—stop and point at an eagle's nest up in one of the distant pines. He's seen the changes around the lake these past 10 years, and he answers some of my questions. "That's Torry Island over there, blocking your view. See the eagle nest? It blew down in a storm, and the birds rebuilt it."

After 3 miles, the Wimp Walk ends. A smaller crowd, perhaps 50 strong, presses on to Pahokee. Some folks join the hike for a weekend; others are in it for the long haul. As the dike swings close to FL 715, we hear the honks of passing cars and see the drivers waving. One car pulls off the road. The driver gets out and climbs up the dike, curious. "Why are you skiing up here?" All he can see from the road are the group's upper torsos and hiking poles pumping away.

Rounding the bend, I get my first glimpse of Lake Okeechobee. The Calusa called it Mayami, the "Big Water" —a shallow inland sea, an expanse of blue to the horizon, broken only by distant palm-topped islands. Scarcely 15 feet deep in most spots, the lake is a favorite of anglers and duck hunters. In the distance, colorful parachutes rain over

Above: Hikers on the eastern shore of Lake Okeechobee
Opposite: Sunrise from Clewiston Park

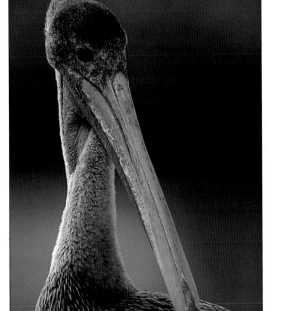

Above: Wood stork
Right: Young white ibis
Left: Pelican

the Pahokee airport, skydivers timed perfectly for our arrival. Tractors are parked under the regal royal palms, and sugarcane fields stretch off to the eastern horizon. Islands of grass wave in the swells along the lakeshore.

Our day ends with a bang: the Grassy Waters Festival in full swing. It's a carnival, a church-run sale, and a county fair rolled into one, where children zip past in a tricycle race, adults gulp down wieners in a hotdog eating contest, and a gospel group sings on the main stage. Grabbing chicken and lemonade, we watch a toy train pass by; one passenger, a young cowpoke decked out in bright crimson, has a chihuahua on his lap. A church group sells "baby Jesus cubes" off a folding table, colored blocks meant to be stacked to illustrate a young Christ.

It's an incredible array of experiences for one day: I went to absorb the hike, and it absorbed me. At the campground, I learn about Sunny's happy hour tradition, where we break out bottles of wine and bags of snacks around a picnic table and sit and chat while making dinner plans. Now *this* is hiking in style!

◆ ◆ ◆ ◆ ◆ ◆ ◆

My alarm goes off at 4 a.m., an unnatural hour. Around me, campers are pulling up stakes, packing their cars, preparing to head to the next shuttle point around the lake. It's a scene we'll repeat several times during the next week. Day 2 takes us nearly 12 miles from Pahokee to Port Mayaca, with a surreal start as we hike past llamas and zebras grazing along the festival grounds. Each morning delivers a spectacular sunrise. My feet begin to notice the dike underfoot, a tough surface to walk on. Blisters appear.

Completed in 1937, the Herbert Hoover Dike hemmed in Lake Okeechobee with its tall levee and flood-control locks, cutting the lake off from its natural flow into the Everglades' "river of grass," as described by Everglades champion Marjory Stoneman Douglas. It's the price paid for security after one of the nation's worst natural disasters. In 1928, the residents of Pahokee, Belle Glade, South Bay, and other small towns along the lake saw a wall of water rush toward them. In the words of novelist Zora Neale Hurston, "And the lake got madder and madder with only its dikes between them and him." These muck dikes offered no protection against the fury of a huge lake whipped up by hurricane-force winds. As one folktale of the local bean-pickers had it, the hurricane "blowed so hard it blowed a well up out of the ground, blowed a crooked road straight, and scattered the days of the week so bad that Sunday didn't get around until Tuesday morning."

The raging waters poured through streets and fields, floating houses and hotels off their foundations and carrying them away. Bodies lay strewn over hundreds of miles of sugarcane and sawgrass, many never to be found. Nearly 2,000 died that day, washed away by the waves. A sobering thought, as I watch the wind whip up the whitecaps on the lake.

At the end of today's hike, we drive to Okeechobee and set up camp at the KOA, a luxurious place for those of us more accustomed to backpacking. With a comfy air mattress and a nearby shower and hot tub, I'm in heaven, although I wince with every step. Paul Cummings, who has hiked the Big O every year since its inception, insists I visit Lou Beauchamp's blister clinic held in the back of her van. Lou, a retired nurse, dispenses advice and punctures and cleans the blisters. Relief is imminent.

Gathered with the crowd at the picnic table, I realize why so many of the people here come back year after year. It's a family reunion, a social event. "It's not just about the hike," says Phyllis, who, along with Linda, seems to hike my pace. "Of course, I'm not the first person to say that." In the days ahead, we become fast friends. With each day's walk complete before noon, we have plenty of time for shopping, sightseeing, and relaxing.

I'd thought, as many do, that there wouldn't be much to see while walking along a dike for nine days. But the character of the lakeshore continually changes. From Okeechobee Ridge onward, we see rookeries and wading birds; someone spots a fox. We pause to watch duck hunters and fishermen coming through the locks; we haul out our cameras for each spectacular sunrise.

Spread out according to our paces, groups of hikers straggle along the dike for a mile or more. Social units break apart and form again as the days go on, often catching up to each other at guardrails and covered benches, great places to sit down and have a snack. Taking a bathroom break is a tricky process. "If you have to go down the dike," says Phyllis, "you have to come back up!" With little to no tree cover, it's a matter of waiting until no one is watching, then getting it over with quickly.

Approaching Taylor Creek, we pass through the site of one of the most significant battles of the Second Seminole War, the Battle of Okeechobee. On Christmas Day in 1837, the Seminoles, led by their medicine man, Abiaka, ambushed a unit of U.S. Army soldiers led by Col. Zachary Taylor. From the high ground of a hammock, Seminole warriors fired from trees they had notched to hold their guns, striking the soldiers as they waded toward them through the

Turkey vultures resting
in melaleuca snags

sawgrass. The fighting raged nearly three hours, felling more than a hundred U.S. soldiers with injuries and leaving 26 dead. Taylor's nickname, "Old Rough and Ready," sprang from this battle. The Army troops outnumbered the Seminoles three to one, and in the end forced the Seminoles to retreat; the warriors followed Abiaka back into the Everglades.

At points along the route, Paul Guyon, who was Sunny's fiancé, leaves a sprinkling of her ashes, none so poignant as at the Hikers' Graveyard. This facetiously named spot has dozens of large granite blocks meant to keep the dike in place. Each year the group takes photos of various monuments written on, jokingly, to memorialize hikers. This year, the memorial is real. I choke up, and blink back tears.

◆ ◆ ◆ ◇ ◆ ◆ ◆

"Did you see the mongoose yet?" John and Pat egg me on at Lightsey's, a great seafood restaurant in Okee-tantie. It's a place where you can order cooter and gator, or a fine platter of Florida lobster. I see the fish tanks. But a mongoose? "Okay, okay." I follow them over to the bar for a look. The things you see on this hike!

As we wrap around past Fisheating Creek, we leave the cattle ranches of Okeechobee and reenter sugarcane country. It's interesting to watch the harvest. A relative of bamboo, sugarcane is a perennial grass that grows up to 15 feet tall. As it comes into flower, the cane is burned in 40-acre parcels to remove the greenery from the plants. The stalks, containing 72 percent water, don't ignite. After the fields cool down, the birds descend, and the dinosaur-shaped harvesting machines mow the stalks down, spitting them into wagons pulled by a tractor. The tractor takes them to the railcars, where the syrup-filled cane is loaded and sent to the processing plant in Clewiston to be milled, boiled down, and refined.

We spend a couple of days camping in Clewiston, so the gals and I have time to explore. Known as "Sugarland," the sweetest town in America, Clewiston is home to the United States Sugar Corporation, the giant of the industry. A little bus called the "Sugarland Express" carts visitors around town to tour the refinery and see harvesting in action.

Because the Big O trek always takes place the week of Thanksgiving, our group assembles at the Clewiston Inn, an elegant historic hotel. I go into the bar for a real treat: a 1945 mural of the Everglades painted by artist J. Clinton Shepherd that wraps around the room. After happy hour, it's a tradition for the Big O participants to enjoy a scrumptious Thanksgiving dinner and the annual talent show, a humorous collage of skits, jokes, poems, and songs by fellow hikers.

◆ ◆ ◆ ◇ ◆ ◆ ◆

It's the final day of the hike. As we start south from Clewiston, the sky lights up in vivid shades of crimson. All week long, we'd commented about the perfect weather, the exceptional coolness that kept mosquitoes to a minimum, the brilliant blue skies every day. By the time we passed Uncle Joe's Fish Camp—where a free apple pie was served, unbidden, to fulfill hungry hiker appetites—I knew that we had a guardian angel.

A wall of clouds now stretches across the lake, a sweep pushing us down to South Bay. I'm half expecting to be met by a TV crew: After all, 23 people just walked all the way around Lake Okeechobee! But we finish without fanfare, just hugs all around. As I drive away from the campground, it starts to rain.

Top: Hiking on the Florida Trail along Lake Okeechobee
Above: Portion of a mural in the town of Okeechobee
Opposite: Aerial view of Lake Okeechobee at sunset

Kissimmee Chronicles

Hiking stick firmly in hand, I wade across a submerged boardwalk as I survey the route in front of me. Rains had swelled the newly defined floodplain of the lower Kissimmee River to epic proportions, a vast and swiftly moving reflective pool of blue enveloping the Florida Trail. I step off the boardwalk into knee-deep water. I push the hiking stick down in front of me with each stride, following the blazes, probing my next step. Going thigh-deep. Waist-deep.

My hiking stick vanishes beneath the current.

◆ ◆ ◆ ◆ ◆ ◆ ◆

It had started out as a simple task: Hike Hickory Hammock, one of the best-loved sections of the Florida Trail. Assisting Doug and Pat McCoy with "trail angel" duties, I'd ferried thru-hikers Sean (who goes by the trail name of "Bodhi"), Ken, and Heidi to McDonald's for their morning coffee, and dropped them off at the trail at Parrott Avenue. Sean started his hike after another grand adventure: He bicycled to South Florida from the West Coast. He'd heard about the Florida Trail when he hiked the Pacific Crest Trail the year before. "It's the hiker grapevine," he said. "Word gets around!" The threesome had been hiking around the Big O for several days. "I'm ready for a change of scenery," said Heidi, "but I'm happy to have dry feet." Like most Florida Trail thru-hikers, they'd waded through the Big Cypress. What they didn't know was just how much water they'd be facing ahead of them.

As I drive to the Hickory Hammock trailhead, the morning fog wraps the ranchlands in a dense mist. This is cattle country, where a 10,000-acre spread is not out of the ordinary. Florida has a long history of cattle ranching, dating back to Spanish colonial times in 1565. It remains the third-largest ranching state east of the Mississippi, with 1.1 million head of beef cattle and more than 150,000 head of dairy cattle. The cows appear like ghosts out of the fog, standing beneath the dark outlines of cabbage palms.

A line of construction equipment sits along US 98 near Micco Landing, where the U.S. Army Corps of Engineers is tearing apart the dikes on the Kissimmee River. Rising in vast, wet prairies southwest of metropolitan Orlando, the Kissimmee River meandered more than any other river in Florida. Along a 56-mile floodplain, the river once flowed more than 103 miles south to reach Lake Okeechobee. What was once a sluggish and shallow river was deepened and straightened for navigability, with dikes and locks added by the Corps to provide flood control after a 1947 hurricane. But the straightening of the river eliminated its natural filtration of silt and pollutants through its many oxbow wetlands, resulting in contaminated water from Orlando making it all the way into Lake Okeechobee. Authorized by Congress in 1992, the Kissimmee River Restoration Project calls for the reestablishment of more than 43 miles of meandering river channel through 40-plus square miles of land.

Letting the river run its natural course means another reshaping of the landscape. I discover this after Doug drops me off at Bluff Hammock and I head south, following the orange blazes to what appears to be the river itself. The blazes plunge in. I take the prudent but difficult route of bushwhacking through tall grasses to follow the river's edge until I can spy the trail again. A tall bridge crosses a deep channel, so I wade out to the bridge to make the crossing.

I can now say I know the Kissimmee River intimately. From the flooded boardwalk, I try several routes to the shore. One is only knee-deep. Looking back at the last 2 miles, I decide to consider my options. I think about Sean and Ken and Heidi. What will they do when they reach the river? My mind switches to thru-hiker mode. It's only 7.5 miles more to my car. Come hell or high water—and high water has the upper hand—I *will* get there.

◆ ◆ ◆ ◆ ◆ ◆ ◆

Above: Barred owl near the Avon Park Air Force Range
Opposite: The Florida Trail through Hickory Hammock passes under live oaks

with rare patches of high ground, such as a beautiful spot under the oaks where bromeliads rain down from the trees and sprout below in mimicry of a pineapple plantation.

When I reach the blue blaze leading to the parking area, I cry. It had taken six hours to hike 9.5 miles. Struggling to change into dry clothes, all I want to do is sleep—a sure sign of hypothermia. I force myself to drive to Okeechobee and have a hot meal. I call a friend and arrange a visit. It took a long, hot shower to lift the chill from my bones.

I did not find out until the day after that the South Florida Water Management District had issued a flood warning after heavy rains near Orlando "created rapid currents and dangerously high flows through the navigation structures located in the northern half of the Kissimmee River." That would explain the drowned trail. Now that the restored Kissimmee River can run free, it will.

Above: Old barn at Bluff Hammock
Below: Oak tree covered in resurrection ferns
Opposite: Lotus flowers float on a marsh near the Istokpoga Canal

Orlando

Permits in order, Rich and I head southbound from FL 520 into Deseret Ranch, trundling down a bone-white limestone road, bleached fossils adding texture underfoot. Deer tracks lead through rain-swollen puddles. A doe leaps the ranch fence to slip into the forest. Moments later, a wobbly-legged fawn emerges. In the distance, a black shape crisscrosses the road in a drunkard's fashion. It's a gopher tortoise, which crashes into the underbrush at our approach. I stop one footstep shy of a thin green snake, which coils up and raises its head in a threat. It's a constant stream of wildlife begging for our attention. And then we

encounter the herd. They watch in bemusement until we draw close, then consternation rules. The cows form mock battle lines, mooing in tones ranging from bugle to foghorn. They stamp and sway, bluffing. Then they flee, breaking formation, scattering across the prairie.

Ascending the levee at Taylor Creek Reservoir, we're amazed by the big sky, the vast sweep of water, a panorama unparalleled in Central Florida. Dead cypresses stretch their whitening bones skyward, cradling the nests of ospreys and eagles. Anglers putter through the shallows, casting for largemouth bass. The levee stretches on for 20 miles, with not a speck of shade. We persevere. Gopher tortoises use the cant of the levee to stake out their burrows. A rumbling cackle and cry rise from a rookery of thousands of fluttering cattle egrets. A red fox slips under a fence.

After climbing gates and ducking under fences, we breathe a sigh of relief when we see the rare stile. Orange blazes lead us to Wolf Creek, where a pine forest swarms over the levee. The primitive campsite contains a surprise—a privy! It's the first I've seen on the Florida Trail. Emerging into full sun, the levee continues past a lake where sandhill cranes chatter on the shore. I look down at my thorn-scratched legs and realize that blackberry bushes surround us. We pause and pick, feasting on the ripe fruit. Life is good.

◆ ◆ ◆ ◆ ◆ ◆ ◆

Within an hour of Disney World, the Florida Trail passes through some of the most spectacular wilderness areas in Central Florida. From the boundless wet prairies south of Lake Tohopekaliga in Prairie Lakes and Three Lakes Wildlife Management Areas, the trail branches into two corridors, east and west, around Orlando. The main route to the east has several alternates. The one we followed heads into the pine flatwoods of Forever Florida, a 4,700-acre private ecological preserve purchased and managed by Dr. William and Margaret Broussard in memory of their son, Allen, who dreamed of preserving this land.

After passing through Bull Creek Wildlife Management Area, hikers on the Eastern Corridor reach Deseret Ranch, an expanse of 300,000 acres where more than 44,000 cattle roam: home on the range, Florida-style. Thanks to an agreement with the ranch, Florida Trail Association members can walk this long and peaceful expanse in lieu of hiking up the roads. Then it's on to Tosohatchee State Reserve, hiking through dark hammocks along the floodplain of the St. Johns River into Seminole Ranch and Orlando Wetlands Park. To get through Orlando's suburbs, the trail follows roads into Chuluota, and then heads up the protected corridor of Little-Big Econ State Forest to the trail town of Oviedo. Following paved bicycle paths connected by snippets of trail and sidewalks through Orlando's northern suburbs, the Florida Trail finally re-enters a vast swath of protected land at Seminole State Forest.

◆ ◆ ◆ ◆ ◆ ◆ ◆

Above: Taylor Creek Reservoir at Deseret Ranch
Opposite: Water hyacinths blooming in Bull Creek WMA

"I don't think this bridge is going to hold."

In the dark floodplain forests of Bull Creek Wildlife Management Area, the sluggish black flow of Crabgrass Creek swirls past. I take a cautious step. Each bridge across this swampy expanse is a balance beam flanked by cables. I make it over the first one. But as I step down onto the next bridge, it crumbles under my feet. I cling to the cables to avoid slipping into the water. The support beam has rotted. Oops! We carefully jam it into position and cross the gap. As we ascend into the pine flatwoods, we encounter pitcher plants rooted in seepage slopes. Each plant sports white-spotted, trumpetlike leaves that grow a foot high and curve inward to form the "pitcher" that traps insects venturing inside. Tiny downward-pointing hairs force the insects into the plant, where glands at the bottom of the pitcher digest the wayward bugs.

Continuing through the palmetto prairie, the trail winds through a landscape that Florida's earliest white settlers detested. Saw palmettos, with jagged saws along their fronds and frustrating "gatorbacks" of trunks to trip across, made it difficult for horses and wagons to traverse this part of the state. In 1840, one frustrated land surveyor quit his job, stating, "This land in its entirety is so valueless that I did not warrant putting the government to further expense." Yet the fresh green needles of spring dress up the cypress domes, and fall brings out a parade of wildflowers, from white sabatia to purple deer's-tongue, peeping through the prairie grasses and saw palmettos.

To the south, the prairies of Three Lakes Wildlife Management Area sport their own fall blooms: the pinks of blazing star, the yellow of golden aster, and the deep, dark crimson of the pine lily. A few inches of elevation alter the habitat. Add a little sand, and a desertlike scrub appears, with sand pines and Florida rosemary. Remove a little sand, and a bayhead rushes in to take advantage of water flowing into the depression, its base a thick, doughy mud. Islands of scrawny cypress form domes that break up the vast expanse of prairie. The footpath is a balance beam of a different sort: a foot-wide indentation in the sand, busy with the tracks of deer, armadillos, raccoons, and bobcats, surrounded by the endless grasslands.

◆ ◆ ◆ ◆ ◆ ◆ ◆

Heading out on a hike a month after Rich and I had worked on a crew led by veteran section leader Wiley Dykes Sr. to cut a connector trail through Tosohatchee, we figured we knew the lay of the land. Because the connector wasn't a certified route, we'd blazed it white. So as we began our hike through Tosohatchee, we knew to look for the white blazes, and bingo! We'd find my car at the end of the new trail.

We start our hike at Orlando Wetlands Park, a model of responsible urban wastewater treatment. The park provides habitat for alligators and wading birds while enabling treated wastewater to be naturally filtered through wetlands. It takes 40 days for the water to work its way through the catchment ponds before being discharged into the marshes of the St. Johns River. The Florida Trail follows the edge of the property around to Seminole Ranch.

In hydric hammocks along the St. Johns River floodplain, we tread through dry streambeds. Along cypress-lined creeks, the water shimmers with the reflections of cypress knees. At the town of Christmas—named for the day the U.S. Army built its fortress here during the Second Seminole War in 1837, and undoubtedly the best place in the United States to get your Christmas cards postmarked—we cross FL 50 and lose the orange blazes. Trying to find them, we come across an ominous warning sign: "Trespassers Will Be Composted." A roadwalk down St. Nicholas Road is in order. Passing a creative piece of yard art, a chainsaw-carved and painted tree trunk, we debate its meaning. I figure it's the face of Old Saint Nick, while Rich holds out for Jerry Garcia.

The blazes begin again at the northern gate of Tosohatchee, where a charred landscape greets us, the Florida Trail sign half-burned and blackened with soot. A wildfire had wiped out much of the pines north of the creek. Tufts of goldenrod and deer's-tongue color the fire-stricken sections of the pine forest, which yields to a canopy of massive live oaks.

As we reach the virgin cypress swamp of Jim Creek, the trail ends. Where is that confounded white blaze? We find a few orange marker tapes in the forest and follow them, thinking they must indicate a trail-in-progress. They peter out. With less than an hour of daylight left and no overnight gear, we have to find a way out, so we head for the sounds of traffic on the Bee Line Expressway. Wading partway into the expansive swamp spreading out from Jim Creek, we decide to leap the fence and walk by the highway berm, a bedraggled pair of hikers surprising the stuffing out of tourists zipping between Cocoa Beach and Disney World. Perhaps they think we're highway workers: Because it's hunting season, we're wearing orange vests. I'm relieved when Rich points down the slope. "There's your car!"

As for the new trail we'd built? We walk in and follow it the next day. Darned if we didn't miss our turn while chatting to one of the hunters we'd encountered in the preserve.

◆ ◆ ◆ ◆ ◆ ◆ ◆

The Florida Trail through the Little-Big Econ is one of my favorite spots, one I've hiked time and again with friends from the Florida Trail Association's Central Chapter. Out of Chuluota, the trail follows a bike path laid out on the bones of the Florida East Coast Railway's Kissimmee Valley Extension, completed in 1914. Henry Flagler meant to open up the swamplands to the southeast of Chuluota, but he had few takers, and his land company folded. The piers of the old railroad bridge across the Econlockhatchee River served to prop up a swinging bridge for hikers, but the

rickety but fun-to-cross span was recently demolished. Beneath the crossing lives the monster of the Econ River, an immense, elderly bull alligator sometimes seen sleeping on the shoreline, a good deterrent against wading the waterway. As the trail rambles along natural sand levees created by the ebb and flow of the river, scenic views abound en route to Barr Street. Between Barr Street and Lockwood Road, hikers pause at a dramatic opening in the forest, where the Econ slides by beneath the oaks.

The Florida Trail heads through a swampy hydric hammock

Strolling down sidewalks, breezing past backyards, wading through thigh-high weeds down a utility easement, slipping on the ballast of a forgotten railbed—it's all part of following the Florida Trail through suburban Orlando. After walking through dark forests heavy with ferns, I feel strange zigzagging between subdivisions as I follow sidewalks and old dirt roads, then squeeze through a narrow gap in a chain-link fence. In a splash of irony, roosters strut past the Popeyes Chicken & Biscuits along the rail trail leading through Oviedo. Eagles nest in a tall pine near the Black Hammock trailhead. Ducking into Spring Hammock Preserve in Winter Springs, the Florida Trail follows the tea-colored waters of Soldier Creek through forests of ancient oaks and tall cabbage palms, past what is thought to be the oldest cypress in the Southeast: The Senator, at Big Tree Park, its 3,500-year-old bulk towering well above the rest of the forest.

It's a relief to the northbound thru-hiker to cross the Wekiva River bridge on FL 46 and enter Seminole State Forest, part of the green corridor linking the Wekiva River floodplain with the Ocala National Forest. It is along this corridor that many Florida black bears roam, leaving behind piles of scat sweet with the scent of grapes. Grown males of this diminutive and endangered subspecies of the black bear weigh around 350 pounds.

From the sand pine scrub to the hammocks along Blackwater Creek, the forest delights. Deer moss frames the trail in a carpet of seafoam fuzz. A zebra swallowtail alights on the broad purple bloom of a passionflower. Clear water pours from a subterranean chamber, freeing whitened fossils and jet-black shark's teeth to be discovered on the bright sand bottom of the shallow Shark Tooth Run. It is a wilderness filled with a variety of small wonders, the perfect gateway to the glory of the Ocala National Forest.

Above: Bald eagle near Oviedo

Left: The Florida Trail jumps on and off deeply shaded roads in Seminole State Forest

Opposite: Vines on "The Senator," likely the oldest cypress tree in the Southeast, Big Tree Park

Next page: Goldenglow blooming in a side slough, Three Lakes WMA

Into the Ocala

A brisk wind blew through the pines as Reverend Sellers slung his haversack over his shoulder. Another month, another circuit, another long walk. From his home in Paisley, he followed the old trails, dodging thickets of red bay and vast flatwoods ponds to the crystal-clear waters of Alexander Springs. From there, it would take him another day to walk the scrub to Pat's Island, where he'd give this month's sermon at the Chapel Methodist Church. He shook the sand out of his shoes and settled down along the spring for an evening's rest.

Ninety years before the Florida Trail Association set its first blaze down at Clearwater Lake, Reverend Sellers and others had walked the trails of the great forest known to locals as the Big Scrub. Dense with sand pine, the scrub relied on fire to rejuvenate, making it a poor choice for human settlement and difficult for agriculture. Scraping a living out of the Big Scrub was tough. According to one folktale, a farmer sold off a piece of poor land to a church, which in turn had to "telegraph Jacksonville for 10 sacks of commercial fertilizer…before they could raise a tune."

It was no great loss to Florida's settlers, then, when President Theodore Roosevelt designated 160,000 acres of the Big Scrub as the Ocala National Forest on November 24, 1908, creating the first national forest east of the Mississippi River. Looked after by rangers on horseback out of their station in Lake Bryant, "the forest," as those who live in and around it know it, contains thousands of small inholdings, including entire towns.

The forest's protected expanse made it a logical choice for the first section of the Florida Trail. In October 1966, FTA founder Jim Kern and a handful of hikers gathered at Clearwater Lake Recreation Area. As the media watched, Kern stenciled on the road the first blaze of the Florida Trail.

◆ ◆ ◆ ◆ ◆ ◆ ◆

"The Florida Trail is like a string of pearls," says Deb Blick. "You have a little gem here, and a little gem there, and all these rough connections in between." I've always heard the Ocala referred to as the jewel of the trail. For several days, I join Deb as she goes about her work. As the Florida Trail Association's trail inventory coordinator, she walks the footpath more than any other staffperson. With a Trimble GeoExplorer 3 at her hip, a plastic-shrouded clipboard in one hand, and a bright orange Rolatape measuring wheel in the other, she eases on down the trail, measuring and noting every marker, sign, and bridge.

It's a moody morning, the day after a storm front has cleared. A heavy mist hangs like a shroud on the trees, reminding me of the Smokies. But this is the Big Scrub. Glistening amber droplets of sap weep from a gall on a sand pine.

We hear a muffled boom. At first, I assume it's a truck backfiring on FL 40, but then I hear a louder boom. Since the days when Lt. Col. Jimmy Doolittle trained his squadron here for its World War II raid on Japan, the Air Force has utilized a section of the forest as a bombing range. Although all hiking trails skirt the area, you can still hear the reverberations from a dozen miles or more away.

Walking through a gateway formed by two kiosks, we enter the Juniper Prairie Wilderness, a roadless zone that was designated Florida's first official wilderness area in 1985. Young sand pines shade our progress as the trail works its way around Juniper Springs, where crystalline waters emerge from dozens of fern-shrouded springs to form the glassy Juniper Run. It's a popular area for camping and swimming, with one of the best canoe runs in the state.

Above: Great egret
Opposite: Oak trees draped with Spanish moss

The Florida Trail heading through scrub oak

As we wind through the wilderness, I'm amazed to see so many open prairies filled with water, each busy with the whistle of warblers, the shrill *shrweep* of towhees, the deep-throated rumble of pig frogs and leopard frogs. Four rotting logs provide a stream crossing over Whispering Creek, and a burbling cascade of whiskey-colored water pours down Whiskey Creek. I didn't expect such vigorous streams in the middle of the scrub, Florida's desertlike habitat, and yet here they are—fed by rainfall and bubbling springs, gushing across a layer of hardpan clay hidden beneath the sands.

I want to see a bear. I've hiked more than 1,500 miles in Florida, and I've yet to encounter a bear. I've found bear tracks and smelled freshly deposited bear scat, but the bears elude me. On the road crossing at Juniper Springs, we passed a sign: "Warning! Bears are active in this area." Perhaps today is my lucky day. As Deb and I break for lunch, dangling our feet above Whiskey Creek, we hear a *crunch crunch crunch* in the underbrush behind us. As we turn to check it out, the creature splashes through the creek. A bear? We'll never know.

Emerging into an area razed by a 1997 firestorm, we find the new growth of scrub oaks rising 3 to 5 feet tall, an ideal habitat for the Florida scrub-jay. Endemic to Florida, this threatened species numbers less than 10,000 individuals, with most of the state's population concentrated in the Ocala National Forest. It's a friendly and curious bird, 8 inches tall and cloaked in bright blue and white. Scrub-jays range across their 25-acre territories in family groups, where the offspring of each mated pair hang for a while to help bring up younger siblings. Although they'll eat insects and lizards, scrub-jays love acorns, and will hoard them as squirrels do: burying a cache under the forest duff, marking its location with a strategically placed leaf. I hear the jays calling to each other, but they make no appearance.

We're in a Lilliputian forest, looking out over the diminutive canopy, climbing up and down relict dunes left from the shores of primordial oceans. Then we descend to Hidden Pond, a campsite every backpacker dreams about: shaded by arching live oaks, rimmed by sweeping prairies, close to a spring with an ideal swimming hole, cooled by constant breezes off the water. Quiet on weekdays, Hidden Pond becomes a parking lot of backpackers on weekends, from scout groups and outdoor clubs to people simply trying to escape to the outdoors. You can find plenty of places to camp in the Ocala, but none so perfect as this.

In the fall of 1876, Reuben and Sarah Jane Long established their homestead on Pat's Island, a high and dry island of longleaf pine in the Big Scrub. Growing sugarcane, corn, peas, beans, and watermelons, they scraped out a frontier existence while raising a large family. After their young son Melvin found a fawn whose mother had been killed by a bear, they allowed him to raise the orphaned animal. He called the deer Dogwood. Years later, Marjorie Kinnan Rawlings spent some time with Melvin's brother Calvin on Pat's Island, and the story of his brother and the deer inspired her to write *The Yearling,* her Pulitzer Prize–winning novel.

When the government offered to buy their land, the settlers of Pat's Island moved, but the Long family cemetery remains. Reuben Long is buried here, as are many of his children, their tombstones fading with age. A side trail called the Yearling Trail leads down through the homesteads.

Rambling past a Florida dogwood tree dating back to the days of the settlement, the Florida Trail continues through the oak scrub. Each oak supports a hanging garden. Resurrection ferns spill from the branches, while lichens in red, orange, black, and white dot their trunks. Wispy seafoam streamers of old man's beard dangle from a lichen crust that looks like spilled and flaked turquoise paint.

After miles of forest, my first glimpse of Hopkins Prairie is a jolt, its ribbon of blue an unexpected line on the horizon. Passing the edge of Hopkins Prairie campground, we hear hundreds of sandhill cranes as they fly overhead,

Above: Sandhill cranes along the shore of Rodman Reservoir
Below: Dawn light on Summit Pond

migrating north. The prairie is a broad sea of orange grasses and blue water, rimmed by the green of the sand pine scrub. Water lilies drift across the open water. Deb tells me of archaeological finds here, the remains of fishing villages and fish traps left behind by the Timucua and their ancestors.

It's a prairie that goes on forever, punctuated by willow marshes, red maple swamps, and a thousand textures of grass. It's also a place of silence, so far away from paved roads that you hear nothing but the roar of the wind through the pines, the cries of birds as they crisscross the expanse. It takes us three hours to round Hopkins Prairie, stopping at every fence post, every USFS stake, so Deb can inventory them. It's an exacting, tiring process, and I marvel that she can keep this up day after day, walking no more than a mile per hour.

"There are days," says Deb, "when I get into someone's car to ride back to the trailhead, and I ask, 'Why am I doing this job? It seems dumb.' It only took us 10 minutes to cover what took me five hours to hike." But as we survey the prairie and marvel at the bearclaw marks in the trail posts, I see the twinkle in her eyes, the smile on her face. She really loves it out here.

Morning mist rises from the pine straw through the tall canopy of longleaf pines as Deb and I continue north into the undulating sandhills of the Ocala National Forest. The understory is open; you can see for miles beneath the unbroken canopy of longleaf, the wire grass forming a soft haze across the distance. It's an excellent spot to see deer and turkeys, which is why the forest is one of the state's most popular hunting grounds. White violets and greeneyes emerge through the tall pine straw. As the wind races through the pines, it rumbles like a freight train. Turkey oak leaves spin in spiral dances across the forest floor. With changes in elevation, the trail rises into scrub, falls into sandhills.

Above: Florida scrub-jay
Left: Boardwalk through a hydric hammock

As I wait for Deb to finish recording information about a road crossing, I step out onto a jeep road amid young sand pines and scrub oaks. My hat tips as a heavy rustle of wings sweeps past—a scrub-jay! Almost close enough to touch, it alights in a nearby pine. One by one, the family members emerge, hopping along the forest floor. They pick up leaves and drop them, cock their heads and stare at me. I'm entranced.

Storm clouds roil overhead, muting the light. I look up through the tall sand pines into a grayscale sky. An icy blast pours across the trail. "I'm getting out my rain jacket," I say. And just in time. As the rain beats down, Deb shrugs, "I left my jacket in the car." She's used to the elements. We press on. I'm glad to spy the blue blaze leading toward The 88 Store, one of the funky, must-see spots on the Florida Trail. It's a store, a bar, and a barbecue shack all rolled into one, and the proprietors love thru-hikers. For a small fee, you can grab a hot shower and pitch a tent in the backyard after chowing down on succulent pork barbecue—a great way to wrap up a day's hike.

Below: Regrowth in burned area, Juniper Prairie Wilderness
Next page: Fern Hammock Springs, Juniper Prairie Wilderness

55

The Western Corridor

Rattling down the rough asphalt pavement, the pickup truck screeched to a stop just a few feet before it reached us. Several bird dog puppies hung their heads out of the truck bed, excited for some attention. The driver, a young fellow with hair tousled by the wind, looked us up and down. "Need a ride?"

"We're hiking," Rich replied, as he'd done nearly a dozen times along this 70-mile stretch of roadwalk. "Our car's just a few miles up the road. No need to worry."

Crimson leaves swirled off the sweetgum trees and fell along the road-side. For January, the temperature steamed, pushing 80 degrees. For about 6 miles, we'd been on Deen Still Road, a lonely, quiet stretch with few cars to bother us. Cypresses, cattle, and orange groves pointed the way toward the Green Swamp.

The driver scratched his head and patted a cooler next to him on the pickup seat. "Wow. Can I get you something? A Pepsi?"

"No." Rich shook his head. Before I could turn my attention from the puppies, the driver started to pull away. My voice came out in a strangled squeak. "What? You turned down a cold drink?"

"I don't like Pepsi."

"I do!"

By then, the pickup was rattling away, well out of earshot down the lonely road.

I t was in the act of trail-building, following Ken Smith's flags through the thick forests on the Marjorie Harris Carr Cross Florida Greenway, that I had first discovered a little-known secret about the Florida Trail—it has an alternate route for thru-hikers! The Western Corridor west of Orlando swings through the Greenway close to my home in Ocala and picks its way across public lands and down roads until it reconnects with the main trail south of St. Cloud.

The Florida Trail Association realized early on that the explosive growth of Orlando would continue to degrade the wildness of the existing trail, so the concept of an alternate route came along early in the planning stages. Jogging up along the southwest edge of Orlando, the route heads for protected lands in the Green Swamp, Withlacoochee State Forest, and the Cross Florida Greenway. Looking it over on a map, Rich and I decided to tackle what we dubbed "The Big 360," an almost-circular Florida Trail route of almost 360 miles around Orlando, using the main trail and the Western Corridor. It took 32 days of day hiking stretched out over a year.

The route is a fluid thing, a work in progress. Like much of the Florida Trail, it heavily depends on land acquisition. Land acquisition specialist Howard Pardue worked with FTA members at conferences during 2001 to define an optimal route. The Western Corridor proceeds northwest from the main trail at Prairie Lakes Wildlife Management Area, hugging Lake Kissimmee as it makes its way to public lands south of Lake Tohopekaliga. Circling west through the open spaces remaining on the edge of Orlando's sprawl, it connects to the Van Fleet Trail near Polk City, providing a route into the Green Swamp. Using connecting roadwalks, the trail parallels hoped-for trail corridors between several tracts of Withlacoochee State Forest and links to the Cross Florida Greenway via the Withlacoochee Rail Trail.

Above: Yellow-rumped warbler on a cypress knee
Opposite: Cypress stand in the Green Swamp

Today's Western Corridor includes more than 100 miles of roadwalk. Tramping along the edges of roads and ribbons of rail trails, Rich and I snaked our way northwest through St. Cloud and Kissimmee. We walked around Lake Tohopekaliga, down the old brick streets of Kissimmee, and along an original stretch of the Old Tampa Highway, buried in the woods off US 17/92. Here, the timeworn brick road, edged by cypress boards, told of an era long gone. We laughed at the error in a monument erected along the road in 1930, honoring the county line with the statement, "Polk County: Citurs Center," and at the artistic statement made by half-buried vehicles in a backyard along Deen Still Road. Passing groves and ranches, we met the Van Fleet Trail, running from Polk City north past Groveland. Following the maps, we went through cattle country until we'd put 70 miles of pavement underfoot and touched our first Florida Trail sign of the journey at the Rock Ridge gate of the Green Swamp East Wildlife Management Area.

The Green Swamp encompasses some 850 square miles of the headwaters of four of Florida's major rivers —the Peace, the Hillsborough, the Ocklawaha, and the Withlacoochee. We arrived in a drought year, so dry that the Withlacoochee River was a series of puddles under the high bridges. The trail through Green Swamp is a backpacker's delight, a 30-mile stretch following the north-flowing Withlacoochee through cypress swamp, pine scrub, sandhills, and broad prairies. Given its close proximity to Tampa and Orlando, it's amazing that such a wilderness as Green Swamp still exists. Fortunately, the Southwest Florida Water Management District realized the crucial role that the Green Swamp serves for replenishment of the region's aquifers.

North of Green Swamp lies the Richloam Tract of the Withlacoochee State Forest, with tall cypress along the river, and slash pines blanketing the uplands. With more than 155,000 acres spread across four counties on numerous distinct tracts, Withlacoochee State Forest is Florida's second-largest state forest, a busy place for outdoors enthusiasts. In addition to its many miles of hiking trails, the forest offers equestrian, biking, and motorcycle trails, as well as fishing, hunting, camping, and caving. The FTA maintains a loop trail in Richloam, which passes by several large sinkholes and through a unique eucalyptus forest.

Walking through a logged-out area, we spied several swallow-tailed kites swooping and diving from the sky. Emerging from Clay Sink Road to walk up FL 50 into Ridge Manor, I laughed at the Weeki Wachee billboard. The Gulf of Mexico was less than 20 miles away! But our route turned north, away from the Gulf, following the roads up to the Croom Tract. Stretching 6.5 miles, the Croom Hiking Trail connects two developed campgrounds, meandering along the riverbanks through floodplain forests and under grand live oaks. As we walked, the sweet aroma of magnolia blossoms filled the forest.

In Nobleton, we headed up the Withlacoochee State Trail, a bike path running nearly 47 miles from Dade City to Dunnellon. Thanks to the bicycle traffic, there are places to stop and take a break: the old-time general store in

Istachatta, the lakeside park in Inverness, the ice-cream parlor in Hernando. Hikers walk by country stores and cemeteries, past houses and historic sites, through tiny, tree-lined towns like Floral City and larger ones like Inverness. Reaching Dunnellon, hikers follow the roads over to the new Pruitt Trailhead, the westernmost terminus of the Florida Trail on the Cross Florida Greenway.

As we walk the mile and a quarter along the Florida Trail through deep woods to the west of Belleview, the low-hanging clouds that threatened the morning with rain now part. Emerging from the forest, we find a crowd of more than a hundred people gathered in a clearing. Thousands of trucks and cars stream past along busy I-75.

It's September 30, 2000, a day for rejoicing. Nearly 10 years after the Marjorie Harris Carr Cross Florida Greenway became a reality, and slightly more than a year since this construction project began, we're about to witness the birth of something special. Something unique. Something Florida can brag about forever.

It's the nation's first land bridge.

It's not your normal pedestrian bridge over a highway. More than a thousand tons of material went into its construction. Two-thousand-foot beams span six lanes of I-75. This gigantic planter—supporting rocks, trees, and shrubs—is odd enough to make motorists do a double take. Tall oaks rise up above an understory of scrub palmetto; limestone walls and fences keep visitors from dangling over the highway. Two overlooks allow the curious to stare down and wave at the traffic. A built-in sprinkler system keeps the plants growing.

Above: Climbing aster with a fly
Below: Cypress trees reflected in Silver Lake, Withlacoochee State Forest
Opposite: The Cross Florida Greenway Land Bridge

The bridge was built to the tune of $3.1 million in a partnership between the Florida Department of Transportation and the Florida Department of Environmental Protection. Recreational groups who use the Cross Florida Greenway banded together to coordinate trail building: equestrian groups, the Ocala Mountain Bike Association, and the Florida Trail Association.

Representing the hikers of Florida, Ken Smith, Joan Hobson, and I help cut the green ribbon. As visitors stream across the bridge, our group of hikers keeps on heading west, following the new orange blazes of the Florida Trail into the 1930s-era canal diggings. Retired Judge William Milton worked with us on this part of the trail, and we follow him down into the thickly forested canal bottom. "Imagine, back in those days," he says, "what a task it was, digging a canal with shovels."

Spanish explorers had dreamed of building a canal across Florida through Lake Okeechobee in the 1600s, and in the 1820s, Colonel James Gadsden presented the idea of a cross-Florida canal in a speech to the Florida Institute of Agriculture. Before Florida had rail lines, the lure of developing a canal route brought many speculators down to Florida,

including the U.S. government. In the 1840s, Robert E. Lee and other members of an Army Corps of Engineers expedition scouted and mapped the wilderness along Florida's shores. But Lee's recommendation for a "canal across the isthmus" languished when the Civil War broke out. In 1887, the Atlantic & Mexican Gulf Canal Company incorporated with the intent of building a canal "from the mouth of the St. Mary's River, on the Atlantic, through Okefenokee Swamp and the State of Florida to the Gulf." But at a cost of $50 million in 1880, the effort failed to attract investors and halted at the planning stages.

Turning their attention to Central Florida, independent surveyors marked a canal route linking the St. Johns River near Palatka with the Withlacoochee River near Dunnellon. By the early 1900s, an earthen dam held back the waters of the Withlacoochee, the first step in building the new Cross Florida Canal. But war again stymied efforts to develop a canal, this time World War I. The project came back to life in 1935 as men took to the woods around Ocala with shovels, picks, and mules,

digging the ditch inch by inch. Backbreaking work kept them employed during tough economic times, but within a year, the funding ran out and the project was abandoned. World War II concerns about German U-boats caused the Army Corps of Engineers to revive the idea. In 1942, the Cross Florida Barge Canal became an official government project. It sat. And sat.

Finally, in 1964, Congress appropriated funding to begin work on the canal. Up went the Rodman Dam, cutting off the natural flow of the Ocklawaha River into the St. Johns. In response, Marjorie Harris Carr, wife of University of Florida zoologist Archie Carr, founded the Florida Defenders of the Environment. She brought together concerned citizens to stop the canal, which would destroy the Ocklawaha and Silver Rivers and cause irreparable damage to Silver Springs. Lawsuits were filed, letters written, petitions circulated. In January 1971, in response to a federal judge's injunction, President Richard Nixon halted construction of the canal. It took Congress another 19 years to put the project to rest. With

Above: Sun setting over slash pines
Right: Abandoned Cross Florida Barge Canal bridgework from 1935
Opposite: Polypore fungus growing on an oak

the canal route officially de-authorized, the lands came into state hands as the "Cross Florida Greenway State Recreation and Conservation Area." With a nod to Marjorie's role in preserving a crucial piece of Central Florida, state officials christened the new corridor in her honor.

With more than 30 miles of Florida Trail complete, the Cross Florida Greenway serves as a key component of the Western Corridor. In the Pruitt section, the trail follows the longest segments of the old canal diggings, scrambling up to the top of manmade levees created by the fill removed from the canal route. Seventy years' worth of forests blanket these artificial bluffs. Heading east toward the Land Bridge, the trail dips in and out of the diggings, an undulating terrain through oak hammocks, sandhills, and sand pine scrub. Dark hammocks provide shade along much of the section out to Santos, where the trail passes through a historic African-American community before emerging at Baseline Road to follow the rolling hills out to Marshall Swamp. From here, work crews will connect the Cross Florida Greenway section to the main Florida Trail in the Ocala National Forest within the next two years.

For more than five years, Ken Smith has led the challenging task of blazing this new trail across the center of Florida. He's been an FTA member for more than 25 years, and an unflagging champion of the Cross Florida Greenway. As section leader, it's up to him to nudge the route through the most scenic and shady spots, to round up the volunteers to cut brush and paint orange blazes and to maintain the trail. "I sometimes wondered why I was building trails to bring more people into such a serene and beautiful wilderness area," says Ken. "I almost wanted to leave it for the adventurers and navigators who wanted to find their way out there, find a place to 'find' themselves." But thanks to Ken's leadership, Central Florida residents looking for a little solitude can appreciate this protected corridor, enjoying the fern-draped, old-growth live oaks that shade this newly christened segment of the Florida Trail.

Below: Cypress and gum tree swamp along the Withlacoochee River
Opposite: Live oaks draped with Spanish moss

Northern Lights

As the Florida Trail leaves the Ocala National Forest on its northward journey, it breaks apart into short, scenic trails strung together by timberland walks down lonesome clay roads through the lightly populated counties of North Florida. At Rice Creek, dozens of narrow bridges carry the trail through a cypress swamp sliced by dikes in the 1700s, when British colonists established a plantation of indigo and rice. It is an ancient forest, dark and moody, where thick cypress trunks sport dense growths of wild pine in bloom. But Rice Creek is only one in a string of sparkling northern lights.

I hear the splashing before I can stop her. "Linda, what are you doing down there?" Turning around as she wades through the burbling stream, she looks back up at me standing on the plank. "Oh, so there *was* a bridge!" Following the winding trail through hardwood forests, Linda Patton and I enjoy the gurgling streams, our constant companions through these clayhills as they swiftly erode their banks, creating deep channels and broad floodplains beneath the tall canopy of hickory and oak. It's an incredible surprise to see the sun glinting off a roof, to find the sign that says "Iron Bridge Shelter." One of only a few shelters along the entirety of the Florida Trail and newly constructed by volunteers from the Halifax–St. Johns Chapter, it's a veritable Taj Mahal, with a covered front porch and two inviting chairs. The structure is open and breezy, covered in hardware cloth and screening to keep the bugs out. At the nearby creek, a 5-gallon bucket attached to a rope makes it easy to fish out water for filtering. This is heaven!

A soft, spongy carpet of pine duff yields to dried oak leaves crunching like cornflakes as we come up to the edge of Etoniah Ravine, an unexpected geological wonder. We peer down 40 feet to the creek. Swirling around horseshoe bends, the crystal-clear water is thick with healthy growths of tape grass. Fragrant azaleas carpet the sloped walls, and dogwoods show off their greenish-ivory blooms. A sand pine scrub creeps up to the edge of the ravine. "It's a fairyland!" exclaims Linda, delighted by the wondrous tableau before us. Copious quantities of deer moss and reindeer lichen thrive under gnarled rusty lyonia. Like green coral, spindly spike moss rises from the bleached white sand under the fragrant silk bay trees.

The perfect shape of the Devil's Washbasin captivates me. It's where scrub and sandhills meet, where still water mirrors the clouds drifting above. Tucked away in the backcountry of Mike Roess Gold Head Branch State Park—one of Florida's first state parks, with facilities constructed by the Civilian Conservation Corps in the 1930s—it's just one of the natural wonders along this brief section of the Florida Trail. Sparkling waters flow down steep slopes and collect in a mighty rush down Gold Head Ravine, slipping beneath the trail in a crystalline flow on their way to Lake Jackson. Clusters of pawpaw dangle ivory blooms against the muted colors of the sandhills in spring, a symphony of earth tones. Young longleaf pines look like a collection of green bottlebrushes. Diminutive earth stars, a form of puffball mushroom, rise from the pine duff.

A gopher tortoise pauses in mid-chew upon my approach. These ponderous, long-lived land tortoises have suffered in number to the point at which they're now a protected species. During the Great Depression, folks around here called them "Hoover's chickens" because they were good eating, and President Hoover didn't exactly come through with his promise of "a chicken in every pot." A cornerstone species of the sandhill habitat, each gopher tortoise creates multiple burrows; the unoccupied ones provide housing for other sandhill species such as toads, lizards, mice, and snakes.

It's a clear day. The distant rumble comes not from thunder, but from bombing exercises at nearby Camp Blanding, a bastion of the Florida National Guard. During World War II, the base served as a prisoner-of-war camp

Above: Volunteers building a shelter at Falling Branch Creek, Etoniah Creek State Forest
Opposite: The Florida Trail passes through a pine plantation near Lake Butler

for German POWs. Although the Florida Trail crosses the base, it's subject to closures. To hook up with the next major segment of trail through the timberlands of Plum Creek at Lake Butler, thru-hikers make their way across Clay, Bradford, and Union Counties on roads; eventually, they'll be able to amble down a newly acquired rail-trail corridor between Palatka and Starke.

◆ ◆ ◆ ◆ ◆ ◆ ◆

Arrive at Olustee on the third weekend of February, and there will be more than a rumble in the air—it's a full-scale war. Ten thousand soldiers met in this pine forest on February 20, 1864, as the Union Army headed for the railroad bridge near Ellaville in an effort to cut off Tallahassee from the eastern half of Florida. A bolstered Confederate force awaited their arrival. The battle raged for four hours, making it Florida's longest and bloodiest conflict of the Civil War. As the routed Union troops retreated to Jacksonville, more than 2,000 men lay dying on the battlefield.

Drawing as many as 10,000 participants, the annual Battle of Olustee is the largest Civil War reenactment in the southeastern United States. For a taste of living history, walk the Florida Trail that weekend through the period encampments, past the strings of stomping cavalry horses and the cookfires with sizzling bacon and simmering beans.

This entryway to the Osceola National Forest is also the site of the first trail segment accessible to persons with disabilities, the 1.8-mile Nice Wander Trail, a loop through a dense grove of longleaf out to a boardwalk along a bayhead. Nine months after attending the trail dedication, I venture across the Osceola with a crowd of hardy hikers on a new annual event called the Great Suwannee River 100, which starts here at Olustee. Trip leader Sam Bigbie looks us up and down.

Above: A tortoise peeks out from its den next to the trail
Below: A new section of the Florida Trail in Rice Creek Sanctuary

"You know, this hike is going to be wet."

I figured as much, so I've got my old running shoes on. It takes less than an hour for us to find puddles spreading broadly across the footpath. One thing about pine flatwoods: The trail is always the low spot, collecting water after a rain. Boardwalks carry us over the known drainages, but they can't do anything for the water that pools after a storm.

All around us, I notice the white stripes painted around tall old longleaf pines. These mark the nesting locations of red-cockaded woodpeckers, a species entirely dependent on old-growth forests for survival. The birds nest only in the heartwood of a longleaf pine upwards of 70 years old. A dribble of sap runs from each nest hole, looking like candle wax but protecting the young chicks and their mother from predators. Early-bird hikers will catch the early birds busy

at work, but we're running too late today for a glimpse of these endangered woodpeckers.

We cross a long boardwalk through a cypress swamp with black tupelos crowding the edge of the milky water. In a grand cathedral of pines, I hear a railroad whistle moaning in the distance. We're nearing Ocean Pond.

Railroads defined the settlement of this area, bringing lumbermen and turpentine crews into the dense pine woods to strip and rip. They cut down the massive longleaf

Annually, Civil War re-enactors descend on Olustee Battlefield to re-create the encampment and battle

trees and dragged them out to the railroad for their trip to the sawmill. They carved notches called catfaces into the sides of the largest pines to collect their honey-colored resin to be boiled down into turpentine and other naval stores. Hidden beneath the footpath in one portion of the trail, near West Tower, railroad ties from a logging railroad that ran until the 1940s still remain, masquerading to the passing hiker as roots underfoot.

During one break, we spy faded pitcher plants in a ditch, victims of the winter freeze, before we rise to slosh across a swath of forest decimated in a firestorm. Young growth struggles to emerge. Since the logging heyday of the 1930s, the Osceola National Forest has been a patchwork of pine plantations and clearcuts, bayhead swamps and cypress domes, where ongoing logging coexists with the preservation of patches of old-growth forest for the sake of the red-cockaded woodpecker, the Florida black bear, and other denizens of Florida's wilds.

As we hike through the Osceola, Walter Schoenfelder makes a profound observation. "The best part of the Florida Trail," he notes, "is *between* the blazes." It's what you see when you stop and pay attention to the millions of tiny details that make up Florida's outdoors. I heartily agree.

Above: Sunset clouds reflected in Ocean Pond
Below: Longleaf pines with an understory of palmettos, Osceola National Forest
Opposite: Grasses and a lone cypress on the shore of Ocean Pond

Song of the Suwannee

"What was that?"

Tempted by warm temperatures and a full moon, Bob and I slip away from camp for a night hike. We pick our way along the footpath, stepping across muddy spots half-hidden in shadow. We pause in awe of a grand cypress, a giant among trees, rising from the burbling waters of Holton Creek. A young bat squeals from a holly tree. A limb rakes my face, and I draw back, startled. Suddenly, a splash resounds through the forest.

Bob stops short. We turn on our headlamps, erasing the night with a blast of incandescence. Something is paddling in the enormous pool at the head of Holton Creek. Our lights aren't strong enough for us to make it out, so we shut them off and resume our walk in the soft glow of the moonlight. I step forward and halt, leaving one foot hanging in midair. There, yawning in midtrail, gapes a deep and recent sinkhole—not at all an unexpected find in this region of karst, a rugged landscape born from eroded limestone bedrock, a hallmark of the Suwannee River valley.

Geology had made today's backpacking trip one of the most satisfying on the Florida Trail. Leading to deep caverns, the stone throats of solution holes gaped at the bottom of trailside sinkholes. A waterfall cascaded more than 15 feet down a jagged lip of limestone, tumbling into the river below. Caught between river currents and the outflow of spring vents, a whirlpool swirled leafy debris like a blender. Ours was a day of strenuous physical challenges: clambering in and out of deep ravines, stepping across babbling brooks, winding up and over the natural floodplain levees, following the undulating landscape along the twisting river channel.

I step back from the lip of the sinkhole and turn on my headlamp once again. Hiking at night has its pitfalls. But to see the silvery shimmer of moonlight filtering through Spanish moss draped from the limbs of the Grand Champion cypress of Hamilton County—it has made those risks worthwhile.

◆ ◆ ◆ ◆ ◆ ◆ ◆

Hiking along the Suwannee requires a bit of gymnastics. Several of us cross a simple log bridge as if we're walking on a balance beam, stepping carefully on the narrow piece of wood. Others opt to hop the stream. We reach a cascade over a lip of jagged limestone, where getting across the water's flow demands a broad jump. Then it's up a steep slope—steeper than any I've encountered in Florida—using natural steps formed by tree roots to reach higher ground.

This is truly rugged terrain. Deep ravines channel seasonal streams down to the river. The river itself, as it rises and falls, creates floodplain channels and natural levees, a landscape of steep hills and ledges. Cypresses perch in dried-out swamps 20 feet and more above the river's channel, their broad bases resembling the spreading skirts of antebellum ladies. The roots tap deep into the waters that flow through this land of karst. To traverse this landscape, the Florida Trail uses a variety of techniques, from narrow log bridges and difficult cable bridges to dropping in and out of ravines, leaving the hiker to make a swift hop over the flowing streams. Campsites perch on river bluffs with broad, scenic views, or along sandy beaches on the water's edge.

This section is one of the most beautiful along the Florida Trail, with the trail town of White Springs smack in the middle. You'll find no Wal-Mart here. This is antebellum Florida, lined with historic homes and graced with country cafes. It's a perfect spot to stop and rest for a while, as did the tourists who came to "take the waters" in the early 1900s.

Rising from the depths of Georgia's Okefenokee Swamp, the Suwannee River winds along a 229-mile course, emptying into the Gulf of Mexico just north of the Cedar Keys. Although he never laid eyes on it, Pittsburgh composer

Above: Opossum, Holton Creek WMA

Opposite: The Suwannee River near the Stephen Foster Folk Culture Center

Stephen Foster made the river a legend, attracting 1880s tourists down to Florida for a peek at its magic. Drawn to its springs and vibrant towns, many visitors stayed. Steamboats once plied the river, making it upstream to the towns of Ellaville and Columbus, busy lumber towns at the confluence of the Suwannee and the Withlacoochee. By the 1920s, the tall timber ran out, and railroads supplanted the steamboat trade. Ellaville and Columbus faded away; the tourists moved on to new resorts in South Florida. Life along the river returned to its slow, easy pace, its deep roots of folk culture preserved and celebrated at Stephen Foster Folk Culture Center State Park in White Springs.

On the third day of the Great Suwannee River 100, our group of a dozen section hikers stops for a well-deserved break. In a surprise to all, we find a beautiful screened shelter set along a sweeping curve of Robinson Branch. "This Is It!" a rustic sign proclaims as it hangs over the front porch with its rocking chairs. I read the smaller sign. "For Florida Trail thru-hikers and section hikers —members only."

We'd seen a good bit of wildlife today, but it was as flat as a pancake: an armadillo, a wild hog, a deer, and cast-off catfish heads, the ephemera of Florida's backroads. In the clay beneath our feet, turkey tracks raced between those of deer. We marveled at a centuries-old oak shading a tumbledown backwoods homestead, and admired the new winter blooms of violets on the grassy berm. Yet, despite our various discoveries on the roadwalk, it is a relief to get off the roads and into the woods, a joy to follow the trail through acreage that private landowner Randy Madison has allowed Florida Trail Association members to enjoy, and now this: the unexpected shelter.

Top: Sunset from the Florida Trail
Middle: A popular diner in White Springs
Left: Little Shoals rapids

Because the Florida Trail is still a work in progress, traversing both public and private lands, it's important to have the generous support of folks like Randy, who opened his heart and home to hikers. Only a few weeks before our hike, a Suwannee River–area landowner of a different sort wasn't informed the trail crossed his property when he bought the land. He barricaded the trail with barbed wire and unkind words. Along the Suwannee River, the Florida Trail is a fragile construct. Some portions of the footpath date back to 1967, but their continued existence depends on the willingness of landowners to allow hikers in their backyards. Without access through private land, we'd never see the Suwannee's marvels: the picturesque waterfalls, the grandeur of the river cascading through Little Shoals, the deep ravines near Disappearing Creek.

Disappearing Creek amazes me. A blue-blazed trail along its shores allows us to witness rapids with hydraulics that pour through cypress knees and cascade into a waterfall, which then vanishes into a deep sinkhole. At the upper end of the blue blaze is a bridge where, one by one, we grab a rope to haul ourselves up the steep side of the ravine. And if that's not steep enough, Devil's Mountain lies ahead. Rising 130 feet above the river, it commands a view unparalleled in this part of Florida. Our climb is a struggle, the footpath slippery and deep in soft mud from yesterday's rain. Aaron loses his shoe, the sneaker sucked right off his foot by the sticky orange clay. A half hour later, we stand on a broad sand beach on a curve in the Suwannee River. We marvel at this river: a place of amazing contrasts, a true Florida treasure.

Suwannee River State Park

The Big Bend

A stiff salt breeze riffled the palmettos on Gibbs' Island as smoke billowed upward from the crackling fire lit under an enormous steam boiler. Inside, water scooped from the nearby tidal channel boiled away, leaving a thick brown crust "nicely crystallized in cubical crystals" on the boiler's iron walls, wrote James Dancy in his memoirs.

Dancy guarded the saltworks along with his Confederate cavalry detachment, spending long days slapping mosquitoes and gnats while the cauldrons boiled. His memoirs record that, "One morning what should appear close in but a blockade craft, a sail sloop, and anchored within less than a mile of the shore." The Union soldiers watched the Confederates closely, but no attack came. Yet. Dancy and his detachment headed to Chattahoochee, to be replaced by fresh soldiers.

Alerted by a Union sympathizer in St. Marks, the USS Tahoma steamed up Goose Creek on February 26, 1864. The expedition surprised the Confederate cavalry, capturing a dozen men and chasing off the workers. Sledgehammers rang against iron as the Union soldiers crushed and broke holes through the boilers, spilling the salt on the ground. The lucrative operation had been making $60,000 worth of salt every day!

❖ ❖ ❖ ❖ ❖ ❖ ❖

Scarcely a quarter mile south of where the Florida Trail crosses the road to Wakulla Beach, a dirt track wends its way through stands of slash pine and scrub palmetto to greet the rising sun in St. Marks National Wildlife Refuge, one of Florida's great ecological treasures. It encompasses vast reaches of salt marsh along the Gulf of Mexico, where land blurs with sea.

Our objective is Gibbs' Island, a hammock of palmetto and pine. Armed with a crude map and transcribed directions from Dale Allen, Linda and I hike down what we hope is the right track. Loggers travel these roads, crushing ruts through the profusion of wildflowers in the drainage ditches: deep-purple violets with bursting white stars for centers, bluish-purple blooms of blue-eyed grass, white-throated lilies with yellow stamens.

We notice an acute lack of wildlife in the early-morning light. No waterfowl peering from sloughs. No alligators creeping through the salt marsh. A woodpecker rattles in the distance, breaking the stillness. It can't be the road that keeps them away, for it's painted with the tracks of deer, coyotes, and raccoons. We revel in the minutiae. Flitting from flower to flower are monarch butterflies, strays left behind from the annual winter migration that colors the saltbushes of St. Marks in stripes of orange and gold. Mating snails with curving lilac shells twist in a lover's embrace. Hermit crabs scuttle to their holes, waving ridiculously oversized claws and parting before our steps like the Red Sea before Moses.

We had arrived at an obscenely early hour to beat the tide. The satisfyingly squishy marsh muck makes sticky sounds underfoot. As the sun warms the tidal basin, sand fleas emerge to worry us mercilessly. Frothy like fluffy marshmallows, young limestone boulders rise from the muck. We walk across salt flats, crisp and white, and then the trail ends. We bushwhack through slender needlerush, reeds with needle-sharp tips, and make our way onto a hammock that forms a peninsula stretching southeast toward the St. Marks River. Linda points: bear scat. We search for the game trail, the trail the deer, bears, and bobcats use to travel from island to island. I find deer tracks to follow out into the marsh mud. A hiking stick proves handy, as the mud is slippery, particularly over the gash where the tide rolls in and out; the water is now a scarce trickle, sparkling with fish.

We reach Gibbs' Island. Scarcely 2 acres, it served the Confederacy by producing salt. The damaged boilers still stand, a silent reminder of skirmishes and battles, life and death, over humanity's most precious seasoning. In Civil War days, salt was crucial for preserving meat and for tanning leather. For the Confederate States of America, Florida

Above: Sand fiddler crab, St. Marks NWR
Opposite: St. Marks Lighthouse, St. Marks NWR

77

salt meant not giving up the fight. During the war, salt became so precious that its price rose from $1 a bushel in 1861 to $50 a bushel in late 1864.

While Union gunboats sat in wait at the mouth of the St. Marks River, soldiers and civilians tended the saltworks. After the water boiled off from the kettles, the remaining crystals were laid out to dry, if the saltmaker could spare the time. Salt would turn white after a few days in the sun, and only white salt could be used for preserving meat. Barrels of not-quite-dry, brownish-yellow salt went by mule and horse over the tidal flats to waiting boats, whose captains played an endless game of cat and mouse with the Union blockade.

The men who sat here watched limestone turn orange and red under the heat of the fires. They chopped down the big pines for fuel, leaving

Above: Blue-winged teals, St. Marks NWR
Left: Alligator, St. Marks NWR
Below: The Florida Trail on a levee in St. Marks NWR

only palmettos to guard the kettles. These aren't your ordinary round, iron kettles, the kind found elsewhere off the Florida Trail. Each of these kettles, at least 8 feet long, has welding that indicates they might be boiler units from steam engines, sliced in half and set well above the tide on a bier of native stone.

Around Gibbs' Island, the salt marsh stretches on forever. But it wasn't enough to protect the men who tended the kettles and guarded the saltworks, which in their heyday produced more than 4,800 bushels of salt per day. Florida's thousands of small, Confederate-run saltmaking operations constantly risked getting spotted by Union raiders, who aimed to destroy the equipment and ruin the salt so it couldn't be sold. If captured, the saltmakers were taken to St. Marks and pardoned. The Union blockading squadron didn't want extra mouths to feed in a time of lean rations for all.

◆ ◆ ◆ ◆ ◆ ◆ ◆

To the hiker coming through the Big Bend, St. Marks National Wildlife Refuge is a special place. It's the only National Wildlife Refuge that permits overnight camping for backpackers. Every October, hikers crossing the central impoundments pause to watch the clouds of butterflies dancing across the wildflowers. St. Marks serves as a fueling point for migrating butterflies, particularly monarchs, on their annual journey south to Mexico. The refuge protects numerous unique natural sites—such as Shepherd Spring and "The Cathedral," a haunting forest of ancient cabbage palms—as well as part of Florida's Civil War history.

Built in 1832, the St. Marks Lighthouse sits at the end of the peninsula. In 1864, Union troops landed at the lighthouse and proceeded to march toward Tallahassee. They were stopped at the Natural Bridge along the St. Marks River by a Confederate force that included a group of young cadets from the Florida Military Institute. Tallahassee remained the only Confederate capital east of the Mississippi that did not fall into Union hands before the end of the war.

Before northbound hikers reach St. Marks, however, they enjoy the unexpected game of hide-and-seek played by the Aucilla River along the Aucilla River Sinks. Dark, tannin-laced water fills massive sinkholes, each one a window into the flow of the river beneath your feet. In this karst landscape wrought of the slow dissolution of limestone by slightly acidic water, the

Remnants of Civil War–era boilers used by the Confederates to make salt, St. Marks NWR

Above: Monarch butterflies at rest in St. Marks NWR
Left: Great blue heron

water flows through caves and under natural bridges, popping up in sinkholes. The trail follows an undulating landscape, providing sweeping views of each sink. The War Between the States raged through these dark swamps, too: Confederate deserters terrorized travelers on the roads around Tallahassee, and a band of desperadoes burned the railroad bridge over the Aucilla River beneath a trainload of Confederate soldiers.

All is quiet now. But following the trail across the salt flats, we remember the long-ago sacrifices. I look out toward the St. Marks River, feeling the salt breeze. How lonely the saltmakers' task must have been, in an age of war, in a long-forgotten outpost, a footnote lost to history.

Below: Aucilla Sink along the Aucilla River, Aucilla WMA
Opposite: Tree island in evening light, St. Marks NWR

Apalachicola

"Where's the blaze?"

I look up as the hiker in back of me splashes forward. This is one of those rare sections of the Florida Trail where you have to keep looking down at your feet—as if you could see your feet. Water the color of coffee with cream swirls in mysterious patterns between my knees. I lost sight of my feet more than an hour ago, and I have no confidence at all that I'll see them again today.

I see no familiar orange blazes in this section. But other hikers struggle forward ahead of us, splashing and stomping along a relatively well-defined corridor of water. Trees crowd in from both sides. Another blowdown blocks my path. I try to hop over the fallen tree, but my foot gets caught in thick mud that oozes over the top of my boots. "This trail sucks!" I complain. A giant sucking sound rises from the water as I yank my boot out of its trap. Thwock! I clumsily slide over the tree as Kent, our trip leader, comes back to check on us stragglers. "It's the mud that sucks," he says, watching the next hiker struggle through the sticky stuff slyly hidden under the sullied water of the slough.

This is the Florida Trail through the Bradwell Bay Wilderness. As Florida's second-largest designated wilderness area, the Bradwell Bay Wilderness contains 24,602 acres of nearly inaccessible hardwood swamp within Apalachicola National Forest. More than 6,000 acres of the bay are lush with titi (pronounced "tie-tie"), a leathery-leaved tree with fragrant white blooms. Three varieties of titi grow in the swamp; the most common is the black titi (also known as a buckwheat tree), which grows to a height of about 25 feet.

Different plant communities radiate outward from the center of the Bradwell Bay Wilderness. The titi swamp forms the core, surrounded by an extensive open hardwood swamp thick with black gum and cypress, loblolly and sweet bay. Within the hardwood swamp, pine islands rise scarcely inches above the surrounding terrain. Breaks in the swamp form alligator ponds. Pine flatwoods surround it all.

◆ ◆ ◆ ◆ ◆ ◆ ◆

Although Bradwell Bay is the star attraction, it's only one experience of many as hikers cross more than 80 miles of dense forest and swamps through Apalachicola National Forest. Linda and I head out one bright spring morning for a gentler experience along the Sopchoppy River, where the dark waters of the Apalachicola bays flow as they drain toward the sea. Thanks to a recent flood, drifts of bright white sand cover the footpath, mimicking freshly fallen snow. It's a strong contrast against the coal-black river, the splashes of pink azaleas, and the peeling red bark of the archway of sparkleberries. Bridges span ravines where cypresses grow. The air hangs thick with the strong fragrance of blooming azaleas. "You've got to watch these ravines," Linda warns. "It's too easy to trip and fall and hit your knee on a knee." Standing still along the riverbank, I hear the gentle burble of the river as it flows over cypress knees and logs. It's a peaceful place.

"Oooh," Linda says, bending back a palmetto frond to reveal a tawny, 4-inch-wide moth with yellow spots rimmed in blue. "Look at this!" Struggling a little, perhaps suffering an injury, the moth works its way farther into the plant. It's a showy polyphemus moth, the most common member of the silk moth family. "You don't see many of them around here!" Indeed, it's the largest moth I've seen yet in Florida.

Where the Florida Trail leaves the slow-moving Sopchoppy to head for Bradwell Bay, we pause for a closer look at what locals have dubbed the "Martian Bridge." As crude in language as the crude scratching cut deeply into the bridge's metal railing, a backwoods folktale tells of a man and his buddy encountering Martians on this spot. "They

Above: Red-bellied woodpecker
Opposite: St. Andrew's cross blooming in pine flatwoods

were green and had scales on them. They drank our beer that we bought in Crawfordville...." It's not great literature, but we find it amusing.

◆ ◆ ◆ ◆ ◆ ◆ ◆

Backpacker magazine calls this section of the Florida Trail one of the 10 toughest hikes in the United States. I won't argue. Having traversed it once on Kent's annual Apalachee Chapter Swamp Tromp, I know I'll never head into Bradwell Bay alone. Water creeps up to my thighs, lapping at my pants pockets. I grimace, take my "water-resistant" camera out of my pocket, and shove it into my sports bra.

Kent grins. "This is the lowest I've *ever* seen the water out here."

"This is low?" I turn in surprise as I hear a splash. Ralph just plunged into a mudhole.

"Yup," says Jerry, who's done this trek before. "Wait 'til you see The Pond. That's where you take photos to impress your friends."

Water accumulates across the broad, flat, clay basin of Bradwell Bay, keeping the forest floor perpetually submerged as the water sluggishly moves toward its only outlet, Monkey Creek. Made up of waterlogged, rotting remains of leaves, mosses, and grass, the mucky forest floor hides beneath 1 to 4 inches of standing water. And then there are the mudholes, like The Pond. These deep spots in the landscape hide under cover of clouded water. Only your hiking poles, probing your next footstep, can warn you of their presence. But your hiking companions will try. "Left side!"

Above: Tree frog
Below: Black-eyed susans

someone yells from far ahead; the brush is too thick for me to see them. "Switch to the right in the middle—" A giant splash ensues. "Aaaaahhh!"

Deep in this thicket of swamp forest, it's easy to get lost. According to oral history, in the 1800s a landowner named Bradwell and his elderly black companion followed their baying hounds into the swamp, where the dogs had treed a bear. Becoming severely disoriented in the titi forest, Bradwell left his old shotgun in the crook of a tree. The men wandered for several days before finding their way back out. Decades later, Bradwell's son Carl offered a reward of $10,000 to anyone who could find the old shotgun. Carl died in the mid-1980s. No one ever found the shotgun.

On a mostly dry piece of land, Kent points upward. "This is what's special about this forest." Towering above us is a centuries-old pine, perhaps one of the oldest in Florida. Around it gather pines of similar girth and size, a 12-acre stand of virgin slash. We've reached the Bradwell Bay Scenic Area, about 3 miles into the swamp. I feel small among the incredible trees in this 300-acre wonder of nature. One slash pine, considered the largest in the world until recent years, had a circumference of 128 inches, a height of 129 feet, and a crown spread of 41 feet. But multiple lightning strikes took their toll; by 1998, the tree had toppled, a probable victim of Hurricane Georges. Measured in 1981, an ogeechee tupelo had a circumference of 162 inches, a height of 95 feet, and a crown spread of 40 feet. One year before Congress passed the Wilderness Act of 1964, the Bradwell Bay Scenic Area was designated to protect these virgin trees. Kent drops his voice to a reverent whisper. "The loggers never made it back here."

To the west of Bradwell Bay sit the abandoned ruins of the Langston homestead. I marvel once again at the tenacity of Florida's settlers to take on such difficult environments. A blue blaze leads from the main trail to this

The Langston homestead

pioneer home made of cypress, topped with a corrugated metal roof. Nailed shut, a yellow door stands out against the timbers as if colorized. The 1800s turpentine community of Smith Creek centered on this homestead, where Langston and his wife raised five children before he died of pneumonia during the Civil War. A gravel path leads to a cistern near the creek.

Beyond Smith Creek, the Florida Trail continues along steep, undulating ravines overlooking the Ochlocknee River. A patchwork quilt of flowering bushes—mountain laurel, wild azalea, blueberry, and Florida anise—creates a textured composition. Jogging around the lip of a steephead ravine, the trail continues to Forest Road 13 to connect with Porter Lake, a smidgen of an old campground, before entering a mosaic of wet flatwoods and titi swamps on its way to Vilas. Bits of corrugated metal, bricks, and scattered bottles under the heavy brush provide subtle clues to the thriving turpentine camp once here along the railroad. We are a long way from the nearest town. No human noise invades the forest, just the strum of the wind across the tops of the pines.

I'm resigned to having wet feet. On the western edge of the Apalachicola, the trail passes through Buggar Bay and Fiddlestring Bay, heading to Sheep Island, Camel Lake, and Memery Island through tangled thickets of titi punctuated by deeper cypress sloughs and wet flatwoods, high and dry sandhill islands and slow blackwater creeks. But I want to see the pitcher plants. Linda obliges. We've seen their rubbery blooms in the roadside ditches, gleaming in shades of lemon and strawberry, but I want to see them up close along the trail. We head down into a bog, looping around a pond where I hear a splash. A young alligator watches us pass. "But you've got to wonder," says Linda, "where's the mama?" We don't linger.

As the trail becomes wetter, the bog plants come out: flat-topped pipewort, hatpins, quivering red sundews, and the object of my obsession, the showy *Sarracenia,* each pitcher plant dressed in its spring finery of draping yellow blossoms. After an acrobatic scramble through a cypress dome, we return to the flooded forest road. It's a tightrope-walk of a swamp slog, as we struggle to keep to the high center between two deep ruts hidden beneath dark water. I dub it the "Apalachicola Chain of Lakes" because it's one huge puddle after another, the orange blazes going herky-jerky around the deepest spots to lead you into more bogs filled with pitcher plants. It's wet, but that's the Apalachicola. What fun!

Above: An alligator takes a peek
Opposite: Trumpet pitcher plants

The Western Gate

Soft shadows cast by a needle palm flicker across the wooden planks of the bridge. As Linda and I step across, we hear the sound we've been waiting for: the gushing flow of Econfina Creek, its black water pouring through a deeply eroded ravine. The stream slips through clay banks, creating interesting formations where water meets soil. Spruce pines tower overhead as the trail ducks into a tunnel of mountain laurel just coming into bloom. I haven't seen mountain laurel in years, and I didn't know Florida had any. Yet here it is, growing in profusion along the creek. Its sweet fragrance takes me back to my teen days in the Appalachians of New Jersey, when my first love gave me a bouquet of mountain laurel and lily of the valley, tenderly wrapped in a wet paper towel to ensure its safe travel home.

Tributaries flowing down steep-sided ravines with white sand bottoms meet Econfina Creek by plunging down various cascades. Our objective today is Sweetwater Creek, which creates a significant waterfall as it rushes into Econfina Creek. Linda backpacked this trail last fall, and she's amazed to see the amount of trailwork completed since then— a distinct footpath, and all these beautiful spans carrying us across the ravines and bogs.

As we follow the trail up and down the bluffs, the views are a delight. White froth floats past on the black surface of the creek, a counterpoint to the azalea blooms hanging above. High bush blueberries dangle green orbs ready for ripening. Beleaguered by mosquitoes, a box turtle sits on the edge of an open spot, surveying the flowing creek.

Beyond the next horseshoe in the creek, the trail goes straight down the creek bank to a most unlikely crossing. Bridging the creek is a broad log, rising from its base along the creek to the bluff on the far shore and paralleled with a swinging cable for hikers to grab onto for support as they cross. Water laps at the base of the log. I turn to Linda and say, "I thought you said the creek bottom was 10 feet below the log." Linda frowns. "It is," she replies. "If the water were lower, I'd scoot across the log. But I'm not walking across it. If you want to, go. But if you fall in, I won't be able to do anything."

West of the Apalachicola National Forest, the Florida Trail threads its way through timberlands to reach ribbons of green, the pearls of public land that punctuate the vast, rolling clayhills of the Panhandle. For more than 18 miles, the trail follows this protected segment through the Econfina Creek Water Management Area, where backpackers enjoy beautiful campsites with nearby beaches and springs for swimming. It passes through Moores Pasture, a wildlife preserve within St. Joe Timberlands, where bald eagles soar above slash pine forests. Inside Pine Log State Forest, established in 1936 as Florida's first state forest, hikers emerge from miles of pine plantations to encounter two sparkling jewels, cypress-lined ponds surrounded by longleaf pines and wire grass, the air busy with birdsong.

Connected by roadwalks through the towns of Bristol and Blountstown, and the villages of Ebro, Bruce, and Freeport, these disjunct segments of the Florida Trail provide a series of excellent day hiking and weekend backpacking opportunities. For a thru-hiker, it's a logistical challenge to connect the dots through the western Panhandle, seeking shelter and water along lonely backroads and busy highways. But for thru-hikers, the joys of roadwalking also abound: a warm, dry bed at the Snowbird Motel in Bristol, fresh cherry pie at the Bruce Café, and all-you-can-eat fresh shrimp at the Corner Café Oyster Bar in Freeport.

However, this is one of those days when I'm glad I'm not a thru-hiker. I take a tentative step out onto the log, relieved to see that it's wrapped in hardware cloth for better footing, and I grasp the cable. It isn't taut. It swings out several feet to my left, and I lurch back. I look at the severe slope of the log. If I were a thru-hiker with my pack on, I'd press forward, even though the rush of adrenaline would be so intense that it could last me a month. But I realize that, as a day hiker, I'd have to cross this again on my way back. And I'd have to cross the log downhill—a much harder task. With its waters 10 feet above normal and running swiftly, the creek can't be waded.

Above: Common mud turtle with a fly on its snout
Opposite: Sand Pond in morning light, Pine Log State Forest

"I'm not going." I scramble up to Linda's perch. We decide to try to follow what's left of the trail on this side of the Econfina down to Sweetwater Creek. A horse trail carries us a little farther before we hit a curve where floodwaters had pushed a tangle of brush across a ravine. I stop short, alerted by a movement in the debris. The dusky coil of a cottonmouth moccasin lies mostly hidden by a fallen pine branch, a reminder of the dangers of clambering across this spill of flood debris. We retreat. The waterfall will be there for us another day.

Above: Evening sky reflected in a pond
Below: Cypress swamp in oxbow of Econfina Creek, near Devils Hole
Opposite: The Florida Trail heads into a titi swamp

Eglin

"It's a bear. Isn't it?"

Large and black, it noses around at the base of a tree right along the footpath. I stop in my tracks and silently point my hiking stick at it. Gary reaches for his glasses as the creature raises its head and looks directly at us.

It's a hog, a gigantic wild boar, easily 300 pounds in weight. And it has no fear. It's blocking the trail. I whisper to Gary, "I wonder if it will move."

We take a few steps forward. The boar shuffles off into denser brush at its own pace, turning to watch us as we pass. After we ascend the hill, I take out my camera and attempt a shot. Glancing back at us one last time, the boar returns to the footpath and heads down the trail, poking and prodding at the pine duff as it saunters away.

Old-timers knew this place as Choctawhatchee National Forest, established at the same time as the Ocala National Forest in 1908. But in 1940, the federal government decided that Choctawhatchee would make an ideal spot to run its munitions testing program, and transferred the land to the War Department. Thus Eglin Air Force Base was born.

An old-growth forest of longleaf pine covers much of the 724-square-mile base, the largest such habitat remaining in the United States. Lone virgin longleaf pines and, in places, whole swaths of virgin forest grow throughout the base and along the Florida Trail. Some of the trees are so old that they were swaying in the breeze when your great-granddaddy was just a twinkle in his father's eye. It's a perfect habitat for the endangered red-cockaded woodpecker, which only nests in longleaf pines more than 70 years old. Bears and bobcats roam the forests; otters and beavers splash along hundreds of small streams.

Recognizing its important historic role in preserving this habitat while supporting its military mission, Eglin has a dedicated Natural Resources Division to manage its ecosystems and to interact with civilian neighbors, who traditionally hunted, fished, and walked these lands. "Eglin is committed to outdoor recreation," says Tom Daniels, section leader for the Florida Trail through Eglin. "After September 11, when all of the other military lands in Florida closed to hikers, I checked with Eglin three days later and we had no problems. For months thereafter, I had hikers calling me and asking, 'Is Eglin open?' It never closed!"

As Gary and I hike the rolling hills of the Alaqua section, we walk down boggy seepage slopes covered in rare, white-topped pitcher plants, and up and down through creek drainages with steep slopes. Beneath the narrow footbridge that crosses Alaqua Creek, swift, clear water with a hint of tannin flows beneath a bower of rhododendron. Hopping root to root, we traverse a titi swamp, the sweet floral fragrance a counterpoint to the aroma of dark, thick mud.

Following a soft, needle-covered footpath, we descend toward the burbling of Hellfire Creek. I notice how small pinecones look like hand grenades. Since the late 1930s, Eglin has been the nation's top military weapons testing reservation. Tom had mentioned that little fact before I visited. "We're in there all the time," he explained, "working on the trail. We hear a rumble, look over our shoulders, and say, 'Was that thunder, or a bomb?' You get used to it. I know some people won't hike in there because of the munitions, but they don't drop bombs on the trail."

The trail lies outside the bombing ranges, of course. Nevertheless, part of the routine to register and get a $5 annual pass for outdoor recreation in Eglin is to visit the Jackson Guard office at Niceville and watch a video on unexploded ordnance, or UXOs. These range in size from small cartridges and hand grenades up to massive missiles.

Above: Emerald spider on a spiderwort flower
Opposite: Abandoned railroad tracks, Eglin Air Force Base

I find it interesting that the model they use in the video is a female backpacker who finds a whopping missile on the trail and hikes back out to report it.

Gary notices square divots along the trail. Could they be from bomblets? He pokes around in one with his hiking stick, and I cringe. "They're too square," Gary observes. "Could these be impact craters?" Thankfully, they hold nothing more than leaves. I see something break into a run, and assume it's a deer until it takes flight—a fat turkey amid the sea of turkey oaks.

For lunch we stop at the Alaqua campsite, a primitive tenting area with soft pine duff that provides a comfy surface on which to camp. As we sit down at the picnic table, I hear a rumble in the distance. Gary confirms. Tom had joked about it: "We call this the land of 'Was that thunder?'" With jets breaking the sonic barrier and bombs dropping on distant ranges, the probable answer is no. Tom described one particular night out in an Eglin campsite as akin to "waking up in a war movie" with the sounds of approaching helicopters, gunfire, and bombs a little too close for comfort. Yet, as Gary and I hike, the air is still—just the sound of the wind through the pines, the chirps of birds, and the burble of the creeks.

◆ ◆ ◆ ◆ ◆ ◆ ◆

The Florida Trail through Eglin currently exists in two segments: 44 miles from the base's eastern boundary to FL 85, and 12 miles along the western boundary to the East River. Between them, along the Yellow River, lies one of the state's most impenetrable swamps. It's where the Army Rangers do their swamp combat training, where soldiers have died trying to find their way out of the tangle of muddy floodplain forest. Tom looks forward to the challenge of bridging the gap with a new section of trail, which he and his crew are building. When completed, the hiking route through the Yellow River valley might prove even more intense than Bradwell Bay. Tom grins. "It will be the greatest challenge yet on the Florida Trail."

Above: Great horned owl atop its prey
Left: White-top pitcher plants near Alaqua Creek
Opposite: Turkey oak in autumn colors, Eglin Air Force Base

Seashore

Millie sees it first. "What is that?" I kneel down in front of the orange-blazed post and look at the aluminum box carefully. It reminds me of an ammo canister, the type often used by geocaching fanatics to hide their treasures. I poke at it and then turn it over. A handful of seeds dribbles to the ground. I pick it up and peer inside.

"Oops. It's a mousetrap." Gathering up the seeds as best as I can, I push them back into the box and return it to where I found it. I study the ground around me a little more carefully. "There's one!" Millie points in a broad sweep. "There's a whole bunch of them." Sure enough, more than a dozen of these aluminum mousetraps surround us, and we'd walked past a dozen more, our eyes too busy taking in the beautiful sweep of Pensacola Bay.

Slightly larger than your thumb, the Santa Rosa beach mouse is one of the most diminutive endangered species found along the Florida Trail. Here in the protected University of West Florida Dunes Preserve, they seek shelter in small burrows, their bright white fur a perfect match with the white sand dunes. Nocturnal creatures, they forage for insects and seeds, with little concern about predators. However, mice that live close enough to the high-tide line are easy pickings for ghost crabs, and those near the edges of the preserve suffer the constant threat of housecats. To the west and east of this protected area, the ideal beach mouse habitat—just above the high-tide line—has been paved over for beachside parking lots, oceanfront condos, and rows of stores.

As Millie and I walk along the trail, we see no mice. But we marvel at the emerald water of the bay, the gnarled trees clustered in hammocks atop tall dunes, the stretches of needlerush defining salt flats. After miles of silent walking, with the sand absorbing the sound of the surf and the wind, we find it unfortunate that a monstrosity of a condo complex looms at the western edge of the preserve, the air alive with the roar of new construction, jackhammers, and power saws. The trail turns to head into the thick of things, joining a bicycle path through residential areas and canyons of seaside hotels through Pensacola Beach. At least there's some kitsch to snicker at: A house shaped like a flying saucer straight from a 1950s science fiction movie breaks up the monotony of the suburban blocks.

As the Florida Trail draws to a close, it carries hikers right out onto the beach at Santa Rosa Island, where sand the color of table salt contrasts with the emerald and teal hues of the Gulf of Mexico. Footprints commingle with the tracks of sandpipers and gulls across shells embedded by the wind. As we walk across windblown waves in the sand, the soles of our shoes squeak like corduroy across each ripple. The sand differs in consistency with each footstep. It's not the easiest surface to walk on. But no other National Scenic Trail takes to the beach, and it seems fitting that, in a state with more than 2,000 miles of coastline, its longest trail should end with an oceanfront view. For 28 miles, the Seashore section follows slim ribbons of public land along Santa Rosa Island, weaving back and forth between beachfront, preserves, and bike paths, headed for its terminus at Fort Pickens in Gulf Islands National Seashore.

Walking past Battery Langdon and Battery Worth, which served as coastal defenses up through World War II, I am reminded of the blood shed along the dunes just a few miles from the trail's end at Fort Pickens. In January 1861, Florida seceded from the Union. Federal troops stationed at Fort Barrancas immediately slipped across the bay under cover of night and occupied Fort Pickens on their own recognizance. When asked by the Florida militia to leave, they refused. President Lincoln considered Fort Pickens one of the most important in the country. After his

Above: Spiderwort, Gulf Islands National Seashore
Opposite: The Gulf of Mexico, Gulf Islands National Seashore

inauguration, he ordered reinforcements to sail to Pensacola despite an agreement between President Buchanan and Florida Senator Stephen Mallory that the federal government would take no further action to secure Fort Pickens, for "the inevitable consequence of reinforcements under present circumstances is instant war." Pensacola proved to be a powder keg igniting the Civil War.

Confederate forces massed and struck back in October 1861. According to an account published in *Harper's New Monthly Magazine*, "In the darkness 1,500 rebels landed on the eastern end of Santa Rosa Island, and attacked Fort Pickens in the rear, hoping to catch it by surprise. The midnight storm of battle was terrible, with its vivid lightning and its pealing thunders. The assailants were repulsed, driven back with serious slaughter to their boats, and breathless, bleeding, and smitten with consternation...." The Confederate Army withdrew, claiming a small victory by burning the encampment of the 6th New York Infantry and making off with guns, ammunition, and cash. Fourteen Union soldiers and 18 Confederate soldiers died. Thus went the Battle of Santa Rosa Island, fought on these sands.

Time heals the wounds of war. Birds now claim the interior of Battery Worth for their own, flying in and out of the windows to reach their nests. As Millie and I walk the last mile of the Florida Trail, we watch a great blue heron preening on his perch along a canal, and scan the dark waters for signs of alligators.

The trail rises up a gentle ramp and ends without fanfare outside the main gate of Fort Pickens. In front of us stretches a broad view across Pensacola Bay to the city. In 1989, Steve Sheridan, a Tallahassee resident, stood at this point when he became the first thru-hiker to complete the entire Florida National Scenic Trail. I ponder the weight of history at this spot, where a simple kiosk marks the trail's terminus. From its architect, William Chase, to Geronimo, Fort Pickens has hosted an array of characters. Today, several children squeal in delight as they watch an armadillo nose through the underbrush outside the thick fortress walls. Sun sparkles on the ocean. It's a great day for a hike.

Above: Interior, Fort Pickens
Below: Fort Pickens, the northern terminus of the Florida Trail
Opposite: Deer moss
Next page: Sea oats spreading on dunes, Gulf Islands National Seashore

The Alabama Connection

Wanderlust.

At the second annual Alabama Hiking Trail Society (AHTS) Conference, shivers go down my spine as I listen to M.J. "Eb" Eberhart, the "Nimblewill Nomad," recite his poem on wanderlust. It's in the soul of every hiker, and it drives some to amazing feats.

Four years before, Eb and I hiked a section of the Florida Trail together. Headed southbound, he was soon to complete a tremendous feat: his second 4,500-mile hike of the entire East Coast. After his first hike, his online diary—and later, a book, Ten Million Steps*—captivated the hearts of hikers; the Eastern Continental Trail (ECT) was born.*

Eb was not the first to walk it. He followed the steps of John Brinda, who sized up the hike and proclaimed it possible. Traveling Alabama roads up to the Pinhoti Trail, the route connects the Florida Trail with the Appalachian Trail, then continues beyond Maine's Mount Katahdin and up the International Appalachian Trail in Canada to its terminus at Cap Gaspé. Eb kept going, to where the Appalachians plunge into the sea in Newfoundland.

In the first 30 years of the Florida Trail's existence, only nine thru-hikers completed it. Eb's inspiration changed all that. In 2003 alone, 24 people began the journey north from Loop Road.

In 2002, Jolene Koby-Burley, "Jojo Smiley," became the first woman to complete the entire ECT. After the AHTS conference, Jojo, her husband Frank "Nomad" Burley, and Gary "Bear Bag" Buffington joined me at the Alabama border for a hike south on the Alabama connector, a new segment of the Florida Trail through Blackwater River State Forest. Longleaf pines rake the blue skies as we climb up and over the clayhills; tufts of wire grass form a fine mist across the forest floor. When we stop for a break, Gary, a former ultramarathon runner, ribs us gals about our strident pace. "Is there some prize money we didn't know about?" We let Nomad take the lead.

Hurricane Lake comes into view, a broad sweep of blue against the pines. I spy restrooms at the campground. My Appalachian Trail friend "Gutsy" trained me well. "Never pass a flush toilet," I say. "You don't know when you'll see the next one." The guys roll their eyes. When we reach the road crossing, they wait while Jojo and I head up the road to take advantage of indoor plumbing. As Jojo fills her water bottles, she points out the "FT" sign at the corner of the fence, over by the dam. "You know," Jojo says, "it's a shame we didn't tell the guys to meet us. We're just going to end up over there in a few minutes." Sure enough, the trail leads us right back to the sign.

On the other side of the dam, stumps and logs smolder amid an ashen landscape. Charred tufts of wire grass poke through the blackened earth like porcupine quills. We walk past a sign that sets Nomad laughing. "Look for Native Plants," it admonishes, with not a green leaf to be seen. The footpath itself puzzles us. How can it be a swath of crispy leaves leading through the forest, when everything else around it is charred? These controlled burns are essential to the survival of the longleaf forest, clearing out the understory choked with young oaks. As we drop down along a levee with a thick carpet of pine duff, Gary studies the adjoining channel carefully. We emerge from the forest, and can see it parallels the Blackwater River. "There was a sawmill here," Gary says. "I'm sure of it." Lumbering was once big business in this region, and crews floated logs down the Blackwater to the Gulf of Mexico.

Slipping across the Kennedy Bridge, the trail follows the river downstream. Each curve of the river cradles a white sand beach; each curve of the trail dips under a bower of rhododendrons. I eagerly await the riverside campsite described on the trail map, and am sorely disappointed when we arrive at the end of a well-traveled forest road. "This is where

Above: Dewdrops on longleaf pine needles
Opposite: Juniper Creek, Blackwater River State Forest

the canoe outfitters drop off clients," Gary says. A sprinkling of litter fills muddy tire tracks next to the remains of an old campfire. "We're not camping here," Gary says. "It's not safe."

Exhausted, we press on, taking the first high and dry spot under the pines. I'm just starting to fall asleep as I hear distant gunfire: a round of pops, followed by rapid-fire bursts. I burrow farther into my sleeping bag. It's a nerve-wracking night. I awake with the cold, rough ground beneath me, my sleeping pad curled up at the bottom of the tent. This slope is more severe than I thought! But when I slip out of my tent, I see a million stars in the sky. There is no light pollution here. *This* is why we backpack.

◆ ◆ ◆ ◆ ◆ ◆ ◆

Along its western route, the Florida Trail branches in the tiny village of Harold, with Florida Trail thru-hikers heading south and west through Eglin and Seashore to the terminus at Fort Pickens, while ECT thru-hikers go north through Blackwater. Yet the idea for a connection to Alabama well predates the first ECT thru-hike. Stated Florida Trail Association president Karl Eichorn in 1977, "Linking up the Everglades to the Alabama state line is contingent on two factors: the ability to get the land and having enough volunteers to blaze and mark the trail." Buoyed by the wellspring of interest in hiking the ECT, longtime FTA volunteer and thru-hiker Rick Guhsè founded the AHTS in

Above: A controlled burn in Blackwater River State Forest
Below: A cotton field just off the Florida Trail, Blackwater River State Forest

2001. Its purpose: to build a wilderness hiking trail across the state of Alabama to connect the Florida Trail with the Pinhoti Trail, completing the southern connection of the ECT. At the conference, Rick recalled the reasons why. "We're part of the group that is carrying on the dream…we wouldn't be here if it weren't for the dreams of R. Michael Leonard, Jim Kern, Myron Avery, Benton MacKaye…." Dreamers who looked to the wilderness as a restorative for the soul.

Wanderlust is a powerful thing. It drives these tenacious folks who walk from Key West to Canada, whose collective dreams will continue to link the Florida Trail to more hiking trails throughout North America. I salute those with the courage, the stamina, and the time to take on such monumental adventures. But for me, and thousands like me, we are happy to hike the Florida Trail on day hikes and in sections, enjoying our segments of beauty, the string of pearls—working toward the dream of a day when the trail corridor is fully protected, the string of pearls an unbroken green ribbon across the Sunshine State.

Above: The Florida Trail near Juniper Creek
Below: Juniper Bluffs on a foggy morning

Afterword

BEYOND THE FLORIDA NATIONAL SCENIC TRAIL: THE FLORIDA TRAIL SYSTEM

"I'm declaring this a no wake zone," said Diane as we hit the first bend of the creek, where tannic waters spilled up over its banks onto the Myakka Hiking Trail. Just beyond, the orange blazes retreated into a dark swamp of black water as far as the eye could see.

"It has to end somewhere," I said, and plunged in. Fortunately, the park ranger's prediction of waist-deep water was unfounded. It was briefly knee-deep. Not long after we reached dry ground, we passed a father and son backpacking on their way home from Bee Island.

"Wet?" I asked.

"Yeah." Both of them looked at each other and grinned. Splatters of mud decorated their pants legs like painters gone mad. "Muddy, too. But the camp's nice and dry." They squished as they walked away, with playfulness in their steps.

We emerged from the flooded forest to a grand prairie, a sweep of open space unlike any I'd ever seen before in the Florida wilds, a vast savanna of tall grasses and scattered pines on a daunting scale. I felt both small and alive, marveling at the expanse. With nearly 40 miles of hiking trail surrounding us, and three days for us to roam, our options seemed limitless. It would be a great sunny weekend in the great outdoors at Myakka River State Park.

◆ ◆ ◆ ◆ ◆ ◆ ◆

When Florida Trail Association volunteers started building trails back in 1966, they ran into a major stumbling block: the cooperation of private landowners. Said Fred Mulholland, one of the FTA's pioneer trailblazers, "When we started the trail through the Ocala National Forest, Wiley Dykes [Sr.] and others tried to continue the route through private lands. Just when they'd get a piece done, a landowner would close it. It was heartbreaking."

Ken Alvarez, a volunteer and park ranger, brought the FTA's efforts to the attention of his supervisors. Mulholland started getting calls from state park managers. "Since I had all these opportunities on public lands, I focused my efforts there." Leading a team of hardy volunteers, Mulholland designed and built loop trails across the state, including the Myakka Hiking Trail. "I had this great core group of people. They'd go anywhere. We'd be working on the Citrus Trail, then down to Collier-Seminole to build the state's only jungle trail, then back up to Citrus, to Torreya…"

Since the 1970s, these volunteers have developed some of the most beautiful backpacking loops in Florida, entirely separate from the planned 1,300-mile footpath across the state. Certified under the National Scenic Trails Act, these distinctive loop and side trails are now a part of the Florida Trail System. Today, FTA section leaders and trail masters serve as stewards of these trails. Across the state, local FTA chapters continue to reach out to their communities for consultation, planning, development, and maintenance of hiking trails on public lands. Beyond the dream of a completed Florida National Scenic Trail, they envision hiking trails that enable their friends and neighbors to immerse themselves in the beauty of protected lands in their own neighborhoods.

Above: Sunset over palm trees, Orlando Wetlands Park
Opposite: Egret against a dawn sky, St. Marks NWR

Mud cakes along the edge of a pond, Mike Roess Gold Head Branch State Park

LOOP AND SIDE TRAILS IN THE FLORIDA TRAIL SYSTEM

- Avon Park Bombing Range Trail, Avon Park
- Bella Vista Trail, Washington Oaks Gardens State Park, Hammock
- Big Oak Trail, Suwannee River State Park, Ellaville
- Bulow Creek Trail, Bulow Plantation Ruins Historic State Park, Ormond
- Canaveral Marshes, Titusville
- Citrus Trail, Withlacoochee State Forest, Inverness
- Collier-Seminole Hiking Trail, Collier-Seminole State Park, Naples
- Croom Hiking Trail, Withlacoochee State Forest, Ridge Manor
- Daubenmire Trail, Flat Island Preserve, Leesburg
- Dupuis Reserve Trail, Dupuis Reserve State Forest, Indiantown
- Fort Braden Trail, Fort Braden
- Hal Scott Preserve, Bithlo
- Hillsborough River State Park, Thonotosassa
- Jonathan Dickinson State Park, Hobe Sound
- J.W. Corbett Wildlife Management Area, Palm Beach County
- Lake Kissimmee State Park, Lake Wales
- Little Manatee River State Park, Sun City
- Myakka Hiking Trail, Myakka River State Park, Sarasota
- Phipps Park Hiking Trail, Tallahassee
- Potts Preserve, Inverness
- Reedy Creek Trail, Arbuckle Tract, Lake Wales State Forest
- Richloam Trail, Withlacoochee State Forest, Lacoochee
- Rock Springs Run State Reserve, Sorrento
- Seabranch State Park, Hobe Sound
- South Fork St. Lucie Trail, St. Lucie
- Split Oak Trail, Narcoossee
- St. Francis Hiking Trail, Ocala National Forest
- Tenoroc Fish Management Area Trail, Lakeland
- Tiger Creek Trail, Babson Park
- Torreya State Park, Bristol
- Upper Hillsborough Trail, Zephyrhills
- Wekiwa Springs State Park, Longwood
- Wild Persimmon Trail, DeLeon Springs State Park, DeLeon Springs
- Withlacoochee River Park Trail, Dade City

Appendix A

BIBLIOGRAPHY AND SUGGESTED READING

Belleville, Bill. *River of Lakes: A Journey on Florida's St. Johns River.* Athens: University of Georgia Press, 2000.

Blakey, Arch Fredric, Ann S. Lainhart, and Winston Bryant Stephens Jr., eds. *Rose Cottage Chronicles: Civil War Letters of the Bryant-Stephens Families of North Florida.* Gainesville: University Press of Florida, 1998.

Bransilver, Connie, and Larry W. Richardson. *Florida's Unsung Wilderness: The Swamps.* Englewood, Colo.: Westcliffe Publishers, 2000.

Butcher, Clyde. *Florida Landscape.* Gainesville: University Press of Florida, 2002.

Carr, Archie. *A Naturalist in Florida: A Celebration of Eden.* New Haven, Conn.: Yale University Press, 1994.

Covington, James W. *The Seminoles of Florida.* Gainesville: University Press of Florida, 1993.

Derr, Mark. *Some Kind of Paradise: A Chronicle of Man and the Land in Florida.* Gainesville: University Press of Florida, 1998.

Douglas, Marjory Stoneman. *The Everglades: River of Grass.* New York: Rhinehart, 1947. Reprint, Marietta, Ga.: Mockingbird Books, 1986.

Eberhart, M.J. *Ten Million Steps.* Helena, Mont.: Falcon Publishing, 2000.

Fergus, Charles. *Swamp Screamer: At Large with the Florida Panther.* Gainesville: University Press of Florida, 1998.

Friend, Sandra. *Florida in the Civil War: A State in Turmoil.* Brookfield, Conn.: Twenty First Century Books, 2001.

———. *Sinkholes.* Sarasota, Fla.: Pineapple Press, 2002.

Hurston, Zora Neale. *Their Eyes Were Watching God.* Philadelphia: J.B. Lippincott Co., 1937. Reprint, New York: Harper & Row, 1990.

Kennedy, Stetson. *Palmetto Country.* New York: Duell, Sloan & Pearce, 1942. Reprint, Tallahassee: Florida A&M University Press, 1989.

Kral, Jon. *Cracker: Florida's Enduring Cowboys.* Fort Pierce, Fla.: Long Wind Publishing, 1998.

Muir, John. *A Thousand-Mile Walk to the Gulf.* 1916. Reprint, Boston: Houghton Mifflin Company, 1981.

Mykle, Robert. *Killer 'Cane: The Deadly Hurricane of 1928.* New York: Cooper Square Press, 2002.

Nulty, William H. *Confederate Florida: The Road to Olustee.* Tuscaloosa: University of Alabama Press, 1990.

Rawlings, Marjorie Kinnan. *The Yearling.* New York: C. Scribner's Sons, 1938. Reprint, Atlanta, Ga.: Mockingbird Books, 1969.

Ripple, Jeff, and Clyde Butcher. *Southwest Florida's Wetland Wilderness: Big Cypress Swamp and the Ten Thousand Islands.* Gainesville: University Press of Florida, 1996.

St. Marks NWR

Ripple, Jeff, and Susan Cerulean, eds. *The Wild Heart of Florida: Florida Writers on Florida's Wildlands.* Gainesville: University Press of Florida, 1999.

Sanger, Marjory Bartlett. *Forest in the Sand.* New York: Atheneum, 1983.

Simmons, Glen, and Laura Ogden. *Gladesmen: Gator Hunters, Moonshiners, and Skiffers.* Gainesville: University Press of Florida, 1998.

Smith, Patrick D. *Forever Island and Allapattah: A Patrick Smith Reader.* Englewood, Fla.: Pineapple Press, 1987. Reprint, Sarasota, Fla.: Pineapple Press, 1998.

———. *A Land Remembered.* Englewood, Fla.: Pineapple Press, 1984. Reprint, Sarasota, Fla.: Pineapple Press, 2001.

Stowe, Harriet Beecher. *Palmetto Leaves.* 1873. Reprint, Gainesville: University Press of Florida, 1999.

Tiger, Buffalo, and Harry A. Kersey, Jr. *Buffalo Tiger: A Life in the Everglades.* Lincoln: University of Nebraska Press, 2002.

Tinsley, Jim Bob. *Florida Cow Hunter: The Life and Times of Bone Mizell.* Orlando: University of Central Florida Press, 1990.

Van Doren, Mark, ed. *Travels of William Bartram.* New York: Dover Publications, 1955.

Weisman, Brent Richards. *Unconquered People: Florida's Seminole and Miccosukee Indians.* Gainesville: University Press of Florida, 1999.

Will, Lawrence E. *A Cracker History of Okeechobee.* St. Petersburg, Fla.: Great Outdoors Publishing Co., 1964. Reprint, Belle Glade, Fla.: The Glades Historical Society, 1977.

———. *Okeechobee Hurricane: Killer Storms in the Everglades.* St. Petersburg, Fla.: Great Outdoors Publishing Co., 1978. Reprint, Belle Glade, Fla.: The Glades Historical Society, 1990.

Appendix B

THE FLORIDA TRAIL AND FLORIDA TRAIL ASSOCIATION

Development of the Florida Trail began in 1966 as volunteers from the Florida Trail Association blazed a 70-mile footpath through the Ocala National Forest. Today, the Florida Trail stretches from the Big Cypress National Preserve on the northern border of Everglades National Park to its terminus at Fort Pickens, near Pensacola. Future plans are for the Florida Trail to head south into the Florida Keys.

Bordered by rivers and lakes, and surrounded by forests of palms, pines, cypresses, and moss-draped live oaks, more than 1,000 miles of completed trail offer a unique hiking experience through Florida's vast range of habitats. Roadwalks connect certified National Scenic Trail segments to create a state-spanning, 1,300-mile route. Together, the certified National Scenic Trail segments, their connectors, and side and loop trails make up the Florida Trail System.

PRESERVING FLORIDA'S FOOTPATH FOREVER: *How Can You Help?*

The Florida Trail needs your support. With a goal of completing the 1,300-mile footpath, volunteers and state and federal agencies are working to fill the gaps and to maintain the existing 1,000 miles of completed trail. The future of the Florida Trail depends on the continuing volunteer efforts and contributions of Florida Trail Association members. Your membership is an important step toward the footpath's completion.

As a Florida Trail Association member, you will enjoy the following benefits:

- Membership in a local chapter, with frequent group hikes and other activities shared by like-minded outdoors enthusiasts
- The FTA's bimonthly publication, *The Footprint,* packed with articles and information about hiking, camping, and nature in Florida
- Chapter newsletters with local events and information
- Access to a schedule of hundreds of FTA-sponsored outings and adventures each year
- State and regional conferences teaching trail skills, nature appreciation, and wilderness ethics
- FTA window decal and logo patch

The Florida Trail Association's mission is to develop, maintain, promote, and protect a continuous public hiking trail the length of the state of Florida, called the Florida National Scenic Trail, as well as other side and loop trails, together called the Florida Trail System; to educate the public by teaching appreciation for and conservation of the natural beauty of Florida; and to provide opportunities to hike and camp.

A modest contribution of $25 (individual) or $35 (family) begins your membership today. Please make checks payable to the Florida Trail Association.

For more information or to send in your contribution, please contact:

Florida Trail Association
5415 SW 13th St.
Gainesville, FL 32608
877-HIKE-FLA
floridatrail.org

International Standard Book Number: 1-56579-480-X

Text copyright: Sandra Friend, 2003. All rights reserved.
Photography copyright: Bart Smith, 2003. All rights reserved.

Editor: Jenna Samelson Browning
Design and Production: Craig Keyzer

Published by:
Westcliffe Publishers, Inc.
P.O. Box 1261
Englewood, CO 80150
westcliffepublishers.com

Printed in China by: H & Y Printing, Ltd.

Library of Congress Cataloging-in-Publication Data:
Smith, Bart, 1959-
    Along the Florida Trail / photography by Bart Smith ; text by Sandra Friend.
        p. cm.
    Includes bibliographical references.
    ISBN 1-56579-480-X
    1. Florida National Scenic Trail (Fla.)--Pictorial works. 2. Florida National Scenic Trail
(Fla.)--Description and travel. I. Friend, Sandra. II. Title.

    F317.F63S65 2003
    917.5904'64--dc22   2003057680

*For more information about other fine books and calendars from Westcliffe Publishers, please
contact your local bookstore, call us at 1-800-523-3692, write for our free color catalog, or
visit us on the Web at* **westcliffepublishers.com**.